EFFECTIVE SCHOOL LEADERSHIP: RESPONDING TO CHANGE

Effective School Leadership:
Responding to change

John MacBeath

P·C·P
Paul Chapman
Publishing Ltd

Paul Chapman Publishing Ltd
A SAGE Publications Company
6 Bonhill Street
London EC2A 4PU

SAGE Publications Inc.
2455 Teller Road
Thousand Oaks, California 91320

SAGE Publications India Pvt Ltd
32, M-Block Market
Greater Kailash-I
New Delhi 110 048

British Cataloguing in Publication Data

A catalogue record for this book is available from the British Library

ISBN 1 85396 413 1
ISBN 1 85396 395 x (pbk)

Library of Congress catalog card number available

Typeset by Anneset, Weston-super-Mare, Somerset
Printed and bound in Great Britain by Athenaeum Press, Gateshead

A B C D E F 3 2 1 0 9 8

Contents

Notes on Contributors

Dr Neil Dempster is Associate Professor in Education at Griffith University and Director of the Centre for Leadership and Management in Education. Neil's current research interests are in quality improvement in schools, and the role that staff development plays in policy implementation and organizational change. His recent research includes two international projects: *The Australian Primary School Planning Project* – a study of the effects on teachers' work of school development planning; and *Expectations of School Leaders in a Time of Change,* a leadership study in partnership with scholars in England, Scotland and Denmark. His most recent publications include Strategic Planning in Schools, with C. Anderson, (1977) in L Logan and J Sachs, *Meeting the Challenges of Primary Schooling* (Allen & Unwin, Sydney); *and Planning for Better Primary Schools* with L Logan and J Sachs (1996, The Australian College of Education, Canberra).

Joan Forrest is a Senior Lecturer at the Faculty of Education at the University of Strathclyde. Her principal area of work is in health education and health promotion. In the wider education field, she has been extensively involved in curriculum development, management and staff development. Publications have been in the health education field and related to staff development. She has had considerable experience as a trainer over the last five years.

Chresten Kruchov has worked with school development and school leadership since 1985. Since 1994 he has been Educational Director at The Royal Danish School of Education in Copenhagen.

Lloyd Logan taught in schools, held advisory positions and lectured at teachers' colleges before appointment to the Faculty of Education at the university of Queensland. He has maintained a career-long research interest in school and professional development, with special reference to leadership and management.

Professor John Macbeath is Director of the Quality in Education Centre at the University of Strathclyde. Over the past six years he has been involved in research and consultancy for a wide range of bodies, including the Scottish Office Education and Industry Department, the Prince's Trust, the National Union of

Teachers, the British Council, OECD, UNESCO, UNICEF and the European Commission. The main thrust of that work is in school self-evaluation, school development planning and school improvement with authorities in the UK and internationally. Professor MacBeath is a member of the Government Task Force on Standards and a member of the Action Group on Standards in Scotland.

Angus MacDonald started teaching in 1969 in a List 'D' school in Glasgow. In 1972 he moved to a Guidance post in Paisley and through senior management posts in Kilmarnock and Barrhead, to Headship in Gourock High School in 1986. He was seconded for two years as Regional Management Training Co-ordinator, and since 1996 has been Head of Service in Inverclyde.

Pat Mahony is Professor of Education at Roehampton Institute London. She has worked for many years in the areas of equal opportunities and teacher education and is currently engaged in a number of research projects exploring the impact and significance of government policy in these areas. Her books include *Schools for the Boys?* (1985), *Learning our Lines* (edited with Carol Jones, 1989), *Promoting Quality and Equality in Schools* (edited with Ruth Frith, 1994), *Changing Schools: Some International Perspectives on Working with Girls and Boys* (1996) and *Class Matters: 'Working-Class' Women's Perspectives on Women and Social Class* (edited with Christine Zmroczek, 1997).

Lejf Moos is Director of CLUE (Research Centre for School Leadership, School development and School Evaluation at the Royal Danish School of Educational Studies, Copenhagen. His publications include *Educating School Leaders – an International Perspective* (with John MacBeath, 1997, RDSES, Copenhagen).

Jenny Reeves taught in primary and secondary schools before moving into the advisory service in Hertfordshire. She worked as a co-ordinator of SEN services and General Adviser in Harrow before moving to the University of Strathclyde as a Lecturer. Her main areas of interest are leadership and management development and strategic planning. She is currently seconded to the Scottish Office as a National Development Officer for the Scottish Qualification for Headship

Kathryn Riley has been a teacher, governor and elected member of the Inner London Education Authority. She is currently professor and Director of the centre for Educational Management, the Roehampton Institute, London. She is interested in how educational change takes places and has researched and written on issues of race and gender, leadership and management. Her recent book *Whose School is it Anyway?* (Falmer 1998) raises some challenging questions about who rules our schools and who uses them.

Acknowledgements

Many people contributed to the success of the project 'Effective Leadership in a Time of Change' on which this book is based. Thanks are due to the education authorities from the four countries involved (Denmark, Scotland, England and Australia) and to other bodies in those countries who contributed – the Scottish Office Education and Industry Department, the Royal Danish Institute and the participating schools themselves who gave generously of their time and energy to the project.

The teams of researchers in each of the four countries who did the groundwork and laborious analysis of data deserve special thanks and especially Johnny Thomassen of the Royal Danish Institute, who contributed so much to the smooth running of the project. The others whose contributions are recognised in the chapters of this book speak for themselves in the quality of the insights which they offer.

The final stage of the book, when all is written, is in some ways only the beginning of a long process of checking sources and references, formatting and proofreading. For their immense help in this I am very grateful to Lorne Greig and Sandra MacBeath.

John MacBeath

Introduction

CHRESTEN KRUCHOV, JOHN MACBEATH, KATHRYN RILEY

In January 1994 in Melbourne the International Congress on School Effectiveness and School Improvement held its seventh annual meeting. One of the themes of that conference was leadership. For the thirty countries gathered there it was a theme of common concern and for three of the countries present it gave rise to plans for an international study which would explore approaches to leadership in Denmark, Scotland and England. The host country, Australia, agreed to join the project at a later date.

What brought these different countries together was a shared concern about the shifting ground of school leadership in a time of economic and social change. While the cultures were in some respects fundamentally different there were clear common trends influencing the nature of school provision and the way in which schools could, and should, be led.

All countries were experiencing a policy shift towards devolution of responsibility to individual schools, emphasis on financial and contractual accountability, development of indicators of performance and stress on parents and public as 'consumers'. These brought new pressures and with them, changing expectations of schools and of school leadership. For people in positions of leadership it posed the question 'whose expectations count and how should differing or conflicting expectations be resolved?'

We wondered how headteachers, faced with the growing tensions of management and leadership, were able to reconcile the conflicting demands on them. Were some better at it than others? If so, what was their secret and where had they learned it? Was a measure of 'effectiveness' in leadership the ability to resolve those differing expectations? To what extent did it mean shaping and exceeding the expectations which people brought with them, realising a more personal vision of what a 'good' school should be?

We were also interested in the permanence and transferability of leadership qualities. Did effective leadership travel across cultures? Did the skills of leadership travel within cultures between one school and another? Between a first and second headship? What lessons could we learn from such a study that would benefit people in post, or those following a career path in preparation for leadership?

We did not wish, however, to conduct a traditional research study in which headteachers, deputy heads and others were objects of the research. We wanted the schools involved to be participants and partners in an exploratory journey. We wanted to acknowledge that our knowledge base as researchers was perhaps no greater than theirs and probably much less in terms of experiential knowledge of doing the job. We saw the sharing between practitioners and researchers and the networking across countries as a potentially rich source of understanding and professional growth.

In some important respects the project design we arrived at was new to us all, and one from which we hoped we would all learn as we went along. What we wanted from the project was that it be collaborative, responsive and evolving. We agreed we would:

- consult with and involve school leaders at all stages, in the design of research instruments, in the conduct of the investigations, in the feeding back and checking out of data
- keep an open mind and a listening ear to what school leaders, authority representatives and other researchers had to say as we went along
- modify, elaborate or change direction in the light of feedback from participants.

Traditionally research sets out its programme and timetable and then puts this into operation. Often it has to meet the expectations of the funding body which has contracted for certain things to happen. Researchers can be jealous of their findings, perhaps because the funding body requires this, and researchers often report their findings only when the project is completed and only once the detailed results have been tidied up and polished. In departing from that tradition we risked presenting 'half-baked' findings to the participating heads and authority personnel and thereby causing unease among busy managers who were looking for more clear cut findings and tangible lessons they could take home with them. We were to find that in fact the tensions inherent in the project design were real and that the frustrations and anxieties had at times to be worked through patiently and with optimism that something valuable would emerge from the other end.

We had agreed that we should meet at least three times as a whole group, sixty people including authority representatives and Danish deputy heads (co-leaders in their schools and therefore included), for workshops and conferences in which we would share findings as they emerged and shape the next stages of inquiry. As these conference workshops were held in Scotland, Denmark and England we used the time to visit one another's schools, to give each other feedback as critical friends and to test our ideas against practice. These visits of themselves provided many challenges to our ideas not only on leadership but on some deeply held educational values.

STAGE 1

Our project started with a seminar in Airth in Stirlingshire in May of 1994. At this meeting we began to frame the project and to lay out the parameters for our future work. One of the end products of that seminar was a publication entitled 'Images of Leadership' in which participating heads from the three countries depicted some of the dilemmas of leadership as they saw it at that time. This document laid some of the groundwork for the study to follow and began to give shape and direction for what we were going to do over the following two years.

STAGE 2

Our initial investigation in the thirty participating schools involved individual interviews with headteachers in all three countries following a common set of questions. These were about expectations of self and of others – what did parents expect of them? What were the expectations of authorities to whom they were accountable? These interviews were transcribed and returned to the heads for comment and amendment. A similar process was then carried out with the deputy heads and the representatives of each of the participating authorities (nine in all).

STAGE 3

These data from the three countries were then brought together and analysed, looking for common and distinctive themes. It was then fed back to the participating heads at a two day conference in Edinburgh. The broader purpose of the conference was to mine the data more intensively, to test its validity, generalisability and practical applications. The second purpose was to plan the next stages of the project and agree an approach that would be informative and useful for all the participants.

STAGE 4

The next stage involved further visits to schools to work with small groups of pupils, teachers, parents and boards of governors, or school boards. With each of these groups a similar procedure was followed – questionnaires completed individually and followed by group discussion, and a card sort activity in which a given set of characteristics of leadership were prioritised and agreed as a group.

STAGE 5

A conference was held in Copenhagen, again bringing together school and authority representatives to discuss findings and examine implications for practice.

STAGE 6

A final conference was held in London to review final conclusions and to bring in the principals from the Australian schools. For participating heads, deputies and authority personnel the focus of that final conference was on the lessons they could take away with them to their schools or authorities that would help them to build on the experience of the participants and to prepare others for leadership. One of the immediate outcomes was a commitment to continued networking and contact and exchange visits. That commitment is still bearing fruit a year after the end of the project with a lively inter-country exchange both of information and visits to one another's schools.

Over the course of the project papers were presented at a number of international conferences, in order to challenge and shape ideas with the help of other researchers. Papers were presented at the International Congress on School Effectiveness and School Improvement (Leeuwarden, 1995; Memphis, 1997), British Research Association (Bath, 1996), European Educational Research Association (Frankfurt, 1997), American Educational Research Association (San Francisco, 1996; San Diego ,1998).

THE STRUCTURE OF THE BOOK

The book may be seen as falling into three parts. The first two chapters set the context for the study.

Chapter 1 reviews some of the background literature on leadership and ideas 'in the wind' taking a somewhat selective focus on heresies rather than providing a more conventional review. There are already many books which do this well. Chapter 2 sets the study in the context of international movements of ideas and economic forces.

Chapters 3, 4 and 5 look in detail at the findings from the study in the four countries, while Chapter 6 looks at the bigger picture, pulling together some of the key issues arising from those data. Chapter 7 raises the question 'Who really runs the school?' and goes back into the data to find the answers.

Chapters 8, 9 and 10 deal with broader themes arising from the study – ethical challenges to leadership, the relationship between effective leadership and effective schools, and finally what we have learned that may have implications for the professional development of school leaders.

A postscript is written by one of the headteachers who participated in the study (and was half-way through translated into Assistant Director of an education authority). It offers his own theory of leadership derived from reflecting on experience as a head, enriched by the opportunity to discuss and test views with colleagues over a period of two years.

The book does not have to be read sequentially. Although there is a development of ideas each chapter is self-contained and provides its own source of reference for practitioners, researchers, policy-makers or anyone with an interest in understanding effective leadership in a time of change.

1

Seven Selected Heresies of Leadership

John MacBeath

INTRODUCTION

The heresy of today is the orthodoxy of tomorrow. That much we have learned from Tom Peters, Charles Handy and all those others who have asked to please forgive what they said yesterday because it is no longer true or relevant. Heresy has always been intrinsically more appealing than orthodoxy.

However, heresy is just as often self-indulgent and narcissistic as it is principled and questioning of inert ideas. In other words, we have to treat heresies with as much caution as we do orthodoxies, because they are inherently more seductive. The heresies presented in this chapter must be viewed as contentious, sometimes backed by a fair amount of supporting evidence, sometimes perhaps little more than assertion or special pleading.

1. THE FIRST LAW OF LEADERSHIP – BREAK THE RULES

In the Civil Rights Museum in Memphis, perhaps the most moving exhibition is a metropolitan bus with a life-size model of Rosa Parks seated in a whites only place. The tape recording tells the story of her deliberate breach of the rules which set in train a spectacular boycott of city buses for over a year, bringing the transport system to its knees and an end to segregated transport. Rosa Parks might be described, in Howard Gardner's terminology (1996) as a significant indirect leader. She was an extraordinary ordinary person, someone with no status but a great deal of moral courage. It took an individual with both status and moral courage to follow her lead and give direction to a movement which was to recast the rules, but more fundamentally to change, or begin to change, the norms and mores of a nation.

In 1975, a McBer research study reported that the single distinguishing characteristic of good leaders was that they were rule breakers. It was a finding with an instant appeal to a whole range of people in positions of leadership. Like all good heresies, it is appealing because it defies the rulebook and reflects people's real, everyday experience. The defiant child in all of us sooner or later learns to exploit the realisation that rules are there to be broken, and that on this path lies social acceptability by one's peer group. But rule-breaking is justified by larger motives too. For organisations to grow and flourish, argue Hampden-Turner and Trompenaars, they must constantly seek the creative exceptions to the rules:

> The integrity of an enterprise, its value to stakeholders, must depend on how well universalism (rules of wide generality) is reconciled with particularism (special exceptions).
>
> (Hampden-Turner and Trompenaars, 1993, p. 7)

Without this creative tension, the danger of universalism is a constant quest for the right answer, the exemplary set of rules, the perfect plan. Remember Passchendaele and the perfect plan, warn Hampden-Turner and Trompenaars, which sent twenty thousand allied soldiers to their deaths in a matter of minutes, a plan designed by generals far from the front line.

For people in positions of leadership, there are clearly pragmatic and political pay-offs. Rule-breaking is the way to get things done and politics cannot be practised without a flexible attitude to the rules. Andrew Roberts (1994), Churchill's biographer, assessing his leadership qualities comments that 'He was a young man in a hurry who always broke the rules. It was a secret behind his greatness.'

'It is better to ask for forgiveness than for permission' has become a motif for proactive leadership in the last decade of the 1990s. It might be argued that the political climate of this period has given a licence for deviance to school leaders. Removing the 'dead hand' of the local authority in England and Wales created more space for headteachers to indulge in creative accounting because that was the only way to survive in a competitive climate. The more schools were required to operate as small entrepreneurial businesses, the more they were given latitude to adopt the flexible rules of the market place. Rule-breaking was modelled at the level of Conservative government with audacity and impunity. Perhaps it is in the very nature of the free market and the entrepreneurial spirit.

In our four country study, it was in old-fashioned democratic Denmark where the politics of leadership sat least comfortably. Many of the Danish headteachers found it difficult to conceive of themselves as political operators, while it was the English headteachers who were the quickest to admit to being manipulative and deceptive in order to achieve the goals of the school. These were lessons they had had to learn fast in the Thatcher and post-Thatcher era.

The differences between Denmark and the United Kingdom are not explained solely by current politics, however. They are also a product of different historical traditions and conceptions of leadership. In Denmark, as in most other European countries, there is not a literature or public celebration of larger-than-life headteachers whose schools are seen as synonymous with individual reputations. Perhaps the most world famous of these in recent years was A. S. Neill, who not only broke the rules but shredded them. His influence on generations of schools, teachers and students was profound, and it is proving a slow process for OFSTED (The Office for Standards in Education) to weed out the heretics and, as their Chief Inspector sees it, to restore order, rigour and conformity to English primary schools.

The story of religious, secular and educational organisations, indeed society itself, is a historical dialectic between rules and mores, theory X and theory Y; MacGregor (1960) distinguishes theory X which assumes that people are inherently lazy and need to be motivated and rule-bound, and theory Y which assumes that people are inherently resourceful and responsible. In Emile Dürkheim's words, 'When mores are insufficient rules are unenforceable. When mores are sufficient laws are unnecessary.'

Rule-breaking has long and honourable antecedents. One of the world's greatest ever leaders was also the first rule breaker on a grand scale. This was to prove a constant source of irritation to the lawkeepers, the scribes, and the Pharisees whose first love was the letter of the law. The New Testament was, of course, a complete rewriting of the ten commandments, replacing them not by rules but by humanly unattainable principles.

2. GOOD LEADERS SET UNATTAINABLE GOALS

Managers set targets that are smart – small, manageable, achievable tomorrow, realistic today and timid. Leaders set targets that are large, ambitious and wholly unrealistic. This a conclusion reached by numerous biographers of the great and the good, among them Napoleon Hill (1928) who interviewed 504 of some of the outstanding leaders of his time including Woodrow Wilson, Howard Taft, Alexander Graham Bell, Theodore Roosevelt, Thomas Edison and Henry Ford.

Among the many examples he cites is Henry Ford's goal of creating a V8 engine in one cylinder block, a feat universally agreed as technically impossible. Like other visionaries, he was singularly uninterested in the how questions. Marconi's friends took him into psychiatric custody when he talked about sending messages through the ether with no visible means of support. Gorbachev suffered a similar fate for almost realising his impossible dream.

These may be somewhat high-flown examples to use in the context of educational leadership. Nonetheless, many would argue that the principles still apply. Commentators from outside the educational world, John Harvey Jones for example, frequently criticise schools for their timidity and low expectations. While such arguments are often subjective and drawn from the world of commerce, the same critics can also point to a formidable body of evidence on the relationship between achievement and low expectations, whether at individual pupil level or institutional level.

One of the Scottish schools in our study lies within the skeletal shadow of the Ravenscraig steel works. It is in many ways a typically industrial, small-town, Scottish school, a community scarred by unemployment with many of its pupils from a background of disappointment and disillusionment. The ambition to make the town's High School the best in the world might have been seen locally as a goal too far, but the school found itself in 1996 as one of seven finalists for the Bertelsmann Prize, awarded by the Foundation to the most innovative school in the world.

Such an ambition is, in 1990s vocabulary, described as 'vision'. In a previous decade, talk of having visions would have been enough to get a headteacher locked up, but visions are no longer heretical. They are *de rigeur*. However, they should operate, suggests Leithwood (1992), within bounded rationality. The flexibility of the 'rational' boundaries is, however, questioned by Svantesson (1996) who argues that in Western cultures we are so obsessed with the rational deductive mind set (much of the blame for which he lays at the door of Socrates) that our own judgement of what is and what is not rational is itself questionable. The person who is so brain-asymmetrical that they are totally controlled by the left, 'rational' side is not seen as 'dangerously rational' but as 'normal'. While, by contrast, people with an imbalance towards a right brain penchant for the fantastic can well end up in institutionalisation, even lobotomisation – as so eloquently satirised in Milos Foreman's *One Flew over the Cuckoo's Nest*.

'Your conscious mind is very intelligent and your subconscious is a hell of a lot smarter' quipped the comedian Milton Erickson. The insight concealed within the joke is the insight of 'working on double plane', exploiting the shadowy powerhouse of subliminal imagery and memory. The psycholinguist Pinker (1994), debunking the theory that it is only language which generates thinking, cites examples of the great intellectual breakthroughs which came during sleep or half-sleep, the alpha-theta state as it is known, when the irrational unconscious steals into the space normally dominated by the sensible cerebral cortex and offers bizarre freely-rising visions which demand to be taken seriously, but rarely are. Luckily some leading minds did take their visions seriously – Einstein, Edison, Faraday, Watson and Crick (discoverer of the DNA double helix).

These creative thinkers and leaders talked to themselves. Nietzsche said that never talking to oneself was a form of hypocrisy, meaning that people who aspire to positions of influence not only need to talk to themselves but must listen to the inner voice too. Neurological research suggests that it is reassuringly 'normal' to hear voices and even to engage those inner voices in earnest conversation. The school of neuro-linguistic programming (Bandler and Grinder, 1979) is built on the singular proposition that it is our self-talk and self-listening which drive up or down our motivation, our expectations, our beliefs, our intelligences and our capabilities. David Bohm (1983), the Nobel prize-winning physicist, sees thoughts as things, arguing that at their most powerful, thoughts defy the laws of conventional physics, chemistry and biology. The most dramatic and eerie proof of this is research into multiple personalities (Ostrander and Schroeder, 1996) which found that people with multiple personalities may suffer from allergies in one personality but not in another, can switch in and out of chronic ailments, can have different memories in different personalities and show biochemical changes in the brain from one personality to the next. These are, in the view of many leading neurologists, a product of inner dialogue.

Hill's (1928) exploration of famous leaders suggests that people in positions of leadership typically make an art and even a science out of inner dialogue. He found that it was not uncommon among leaders to have a fantasy board of directors, inner consultants to whom they could go for advice and guidance – essentially a secular version of the inner god or spiritual guru.

Self-talk is a well-known feature of winning athletes and sportspeople. It is commonly referred to as 'psyching yourself up', a process now better understood by psychologists and neurologists. Its most vivid proponent, whose self-talk came to be shared with a global public, was Muhammed Ali. It was Ali who gave us the concept of 'future history' – the process of recording the future before it happens.

The Greeks had a name for this. They called it 'hubris' – having pretensions to be higher than the gods who, after all, had the sole licence to shape the future. Yet we are surrounded by the physical manifestations of those who thought up the future – from the wheel to the mobile phone, pre-conceived fantasies which changed people and their relationships for ever.

We might summarise this second heresy as a willingness to believe in the inexplicable and to embrace the possibilities of the impossible.

3. THE TRUE LEADER IS ALWAYS LED

Carl Jung said that the true leader is always led. He was referring both to internal listening and to listening to others. The good leader listens to those around him or her, knows who they are and is sensitive to nuance and feeling. Good leaders are, in short, excellent followers.

The word 'leadership' conjures up images of those larger than life figures who revelled in power, who took every opportunity to remind people of their status, and who enhanced their own authority by diminishing that of others. Canny leaders appointed as their deputies people who were smaller than them (often in a physical as well as a psychological sense). Julius Caesar asked for men around him who were fat and well fed. Referring to disabled organisations, Peter Senge (1990, p. 18) warned that 'nothing fails like success'.

Life for the Caesars was a precarious path, and holding on to leadership a matter of keeping a sharp eye out for potential usurpers. This was, and still is, true of dictators, generals, presidents and prime ministers. It is even true of education ministers who have been known to instruct their civil servants not to share briefings with other government ministers in the belief that they are the enemy within. A paranoid fear of your own colleagues is true of many organisational leaders, including people in positions of educational leadership in schools and education authorities. One of the most powerful educational leaders in the United Kingdom admitted to a policy of 'constructive destabilisation' – an emotional shuttling of his staff between censure and fulsome praise, between job satisfaction and job threat. This meant that people were never settled emotionally for long enough to threaten the director's power.

His counterpart in another British education authority is widely revered not only for his visionary qualities but for his generosity, his willingness to give other people their place, to listen, and to learn. Tim Brighouse, Director of Education in Birmingham city authority, is an exemplary lifelong learner. One of his favourite expressions is 'being surprised into achievement'. It finds an echo in Hampden-Turner and Trompenaars's discussion of what participation means:

> participation is not a technique designed to get workers to do what their managers wanted in the first place, but a willingness to be surprised by an unforeseen initiative or suggestion.
>
> (Hampden-Turner and Trompenaar, 1993 p. 28))

Samuel Johnson said that there is nothing noble in being superior to some other man, true nobility is in being superior to your previous self. In other words, it is an ability to learn and grow, rather than being disabled and diminished by power. The director who believes in constructive destabilisation provides neither inspiration nor modelling, thereby failing one of the key tests of good leadership – preparing others to exercise it. It might be argued that the Thatcherite qualities of singular vision did, in fact, enhance the ability of many leaders to achieve what they did, but it may also be seen as a tragic flaw which limited their potential for true greatness. In the words of one of her closest ministerial colleagues, Kenneth Baker, Thatcher was 'personally dominant, supremely self-confident, infuriatingly stubborn, a strange mixture of broad views and narrow prejudices' (Webster, 1990, p. 7). These contained both the seeds of her elevation to power and her secretly-conspired downfall.

After the Second World War, the psychologist Adorno (1950) looked for explanations of the relationship between leadership and followership. He developed the now well-known F scale to measure fascistic, or highly authoritarian, traits and identified a cluster of characteristics which constitute the 'authoritarian personality'. Denigration of inferiors went hand-in-hand with deference to superiors. Frightening confirmation was offered by Stanley Milgram's later studies (1974) of a widespread willingness to submit to the authority of others. He found that:

> those who score high on the scale that measures fascistic tendencies crave organisation and order above all; those with modest scores on this scale, are comfortable with, or even look for, a degree of chaos, inconsistency and contradictory minutiae.

It is difficult to apply the term 'good' in either a moral or functional sense to leaders who have no capacity to accept followership. Following the lead of others, suggests Stephen Covey (1994), requires self-assurance of the highest quality. It requires the exercise of the fifth of his seven principles of effectiveness – 'seek first to understand before seeking to be understood'. In our own study, pupils, parents and teachers were agreed on one thing – the primary quality of 'good' headteachers was the ability to listen.

Closely aligned to the art of listening is the art of reading. Cave and Wilkinson (1997) identified four higher order skills in school leaders. These were reading the situation, intuition, balanced judgement and political acumen. Reading the situation was described by headteachers in their study in terms of keeping antennae out and picking up vibes. These are both metaphors rather than dissectable behavioural competencies, but the intuition which underpins these does not come out of the ether, nor just from the gut, although it is often expressed there. It is drawn from a bank of experience and learned by matching past experiences to new ones by neural pathways which connect the gut response to the accumulated databank. In the databank are stored a collection of archival theories of human behaviour.

Conventional theories of leadership start from the premise that the leader is 'in front' or 'on top'. The image below reflects this conventional imagery. It is one headteacher's representation of her job. It shows her pulling people, some reluctantly, up a hill. Leading from the back is a less obvious idea, but one that is neatly illustrated in David Hopkins's (1992) alternative metaphor. He believes that good schools are sailed rather than driven, evoking an image of the yacht being steered from the stern, tacking and changing with a reading of wind and current.

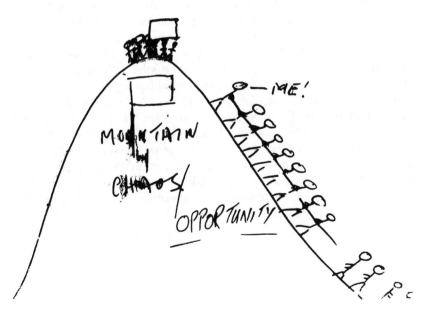

Leaders lead not from the apex of the pyramid but from the centre of the web of human relationships, states Murphy (1994). Leaders are in the thick of the action, agrees Leithwood (1992). It is in the thick of the action that the qualities of leadership receive their sternest test. In a study (Senge, 1990) of telephone engineers who were obliged to work in teams because no one individually had sufficient expertise, team members were asked to identify other team members as 'stars'. While the researchers found very little difference between those who were nominated as 'stars' and those who were not, there was one single distinguishing characteristic which separated the stars from the rest; this was networking. The stars received more requests for help and advice than others. They had, in the researchers' words, 'thick connections', cultivated through listening, seeing the perspective of others, and due to their ability to build co-operation:

> In a learning organisation leaders may start by pursuing their own vision, but as they listen carefully to others' visions they begin to see that their own personal vision is part of something larger. This does not diminish any leader's sense of responsibility for the vision – if anything it deepens it.
>
> (Senge, 1990, p. 352)

Goleman (1996) describes leaders as at the node of three kinds of networks – expertise, communication and trust. He argues, however, that being an expert is, in most leadership situations, of little use without the trust network. While being able to trust your leader may in some circumstances be at less of a premium than high level expertise, the 'McBroom syndrome' should serve as a warning to experts who do not listen or who make trust difficult. McBroom was an airline pilot who crashed his plane killing ten people because, in Goleman's words (1996, p. 148) 'his crew co-pilots were so fearful of McBroom's wrath that they said nothing, even as disaster loomed'.

Why is it, ask Argyris and Schon (1978), that organisations cannot seem to learn what everyone knows? Their answer – because they lack the tools. The tools which help organisations, teachers and school leaders are tools of self-evaluation which become so routinised and imbedded within the way an organisation works that it cannot fall prey to the McBroom syndrome.

Why is it that organisations cannot seem to learn what everyone knows? Covey's (1994) answer – because they lack the trust. Covey puts at the heart of organisational effectiveness trustworthiness at the personal level, trust at the inter-personal level, and alignment (or integrity) at the managerial level.

Putting these two answers together, leaders can afford to be led by the organisation that is not only trustworthy but has the tools to hold its members mutually and externally accountable.

4. LEADERS NEED TO BE STRICTLY MANAGED

As we have learned from history, it is dangerous to give too much freedom to leaders. The more spontaneous and creative they are the more precarious the line they walk between fantasy and reality, order and chaos. Henry Mintzberg (1994), one of the most influential of heretics in this field, argued that leaders operate on a non-rational model, on a combination of data, gossip, best-guessing and hunch. They spend much of their time on the edge of chaos, coping with crises, the left hand initiating change while with the right they are disturbance handlers, responding to problems and making instant pragmatic decisions. Leaders are admonished to be risk takers, to have the courage to fail, to learn from mistakes. 'Failure is in a sense the highway to success', said the poet Keats, a century in advance of Tom Peters and others whose celebration of chaos assumes that there are people capable of imposing structure and order.

It is also argued that the mark of good leaders is that they do not respond to the 'tyranny of the urgent'. They can, by virtue of their status, afford to take the long view, in the knowledge that someone else is in charge of the urgent. This is increasingly apposite in an educational context where there are two conflicting forces at work – the imperative of change and the diminishing of resources to make change happen. The prescient leader embraces change and works to make it happen, but only by making greater demands on his people with fewer resources to support their work, thereby stretching the goodwill, energy and competence of subordinate staff. The greater the demands placed on staff the less able they are to cope with chaos and the greater their need for stability and structure.

The good leader, it is argued therefore, recognises his or her need to manage. This job often falls to the faithful secretary who, if she can make herself indispensable enough, can manage by threat, withdrawal of privilege and work to rule when the boss moves too far out of line. If the old aphorism is true, that behind every successful man is a woman, it applies with equal force to leaders in government, business, universities, colleges and schools. Nine times out of ten the politician's, chief executive's or headteacher's secretary is a woman whose informal behind-the-scenes role is to carefully stage manage things to make the leader look good – on time for appointments, well-briefed, in touch. The faithful secretary discreetly manages the lost umbrellas, glasses, diaries, double bookings and missed appointments, making necessity appear a virtue in the public eye. The high profile work in private is matched by public self-effacement, and the loyalty of the secretary usually extends to not writing her memoirs. So the literature on the driving force behind effective leadership is sparser than it might be.

But it is very often the secretary who has the most acute insight into the driving force, dynamics and underlife of the organisation yet is excluded from management team meetings and organisational decision-making. Her opinion is only sought casually and carries no formal status. Peter Senge (1990), who defines seven organisational learning disabilities, cites as number one, 'I am my position'. Organisations fail to learn what everyone knows because people speak from and through positions – I speak as 'only the secretary', the caretaker, a junior member of staff, the union spokesperson, the managing director, the headteacher.

Burt Nanus (1992), in his list of differences between managers and leaders, says that 'managers ask how and leaders ask why'. Why and how questions are, of course, both essential and complementary, and underline the need for teamwork which brings balance and synergy to the contributions of individuals. The word 'team' evokes a sporting image, and nowhere is the lesson more obvious than in professional football where a club can spend thirty to forty million pounds on a handful of outstanding, creative individual players but lose games to teams who have fewer stars but who know how to complement and enhance one another's skills. Creative players are typically managed by less-gifted captains, managers and coaches. Why is it, asks Nanus, that people with an I.Q. of 140 frequently end up working for people with an I.Q. of 100? Because it is the not the capacities, or attainments, which I.Q. measures that are valuable in situations requiring leadership.

Organisations learn through open dialogue which is not blinkered by positional status, says Senge (1990). Good leaders recognise the need to be reined in and held accountable. The most perspicacious among them realise that this may curb their power but will enhance, rather than diminish, their status. It is becoming more commonplace for managers in large corporate organisations, and increasingly in schools, to ask staff (sometimes parents and pupils too) to evaluate their leadership qualities and performance.

Intelligence is a collective phenomenon says David Bohm (1983). By this argument the intelligence of leadership can only be realised through synergy. The leader receives 'added-value' through those who manage him or her, either accepting that it is an extension of his or her persona, or taking pains to credit the team nature of the accomplishment. Like the Oscar winner who thanks everyone without whom it would not have been possible, it is the leader who still walks off with the trophy.

5. GOOD LEADERS BEHAVE LIKE GROWN-UPS

The history of world leaders is strewn with examples of people who never grew up. Their adult years were spent compensating for the inadequacy of their childhood, never having successfully made it through the egocentric phase or come to terms with the expectations of their parents.

The work of Eric Berne and other transactional analysts has made a major contribution to our understanding of the people we are – a schizophrenic combination of child, adult and parent. Neither child nor parents leave us during our adult lifetime, and in our dotage they reappear in their strongest form to review, reprimand and sometimes to reward us for the quality of our lives. They are versions of the id and the superego, pushing and pulling us to behave and to misbehave, struggling to release the child and to liberate the adult, both in danger of being overwhelmed by the parent.

In their book on Superlearning, Ostrander and Schroeder (1996) quote someone who had tried to cope with the demons of the superego by repeating a nightly affirmation that she was a good and capable person. She awoke one morning to hear a disembodied voice telling her, 'Forget all that, you are really a shit'.

Where did that voice with a life of its own come from? Those voices and images that come to us at the edge of sleep (the hypnagogic state as it is known) are a surprise and often a shock because they are not under conscious control. They are the voice of what Mead (1934) called 'the internalised other'. The 'internalised other' is always someone of particular significance, very typically a parent or teacher, and typically from a critical stage in childhood.

The leadership literature is revealing on the subject of leaders, driven by their parents – a lifelong quest to prove themselves, either to their real parents or the vestigial parent still in psychological residence. Margaret Thatcher's parents, or at least one of them, was a source of both inspiration and inhibition. Her father, the grocer, gave her the model of how an economy should be run. According to one biographer (Webster, 1990) she was never able to put her father in his place nor give her mother her's. 'Most roads lead to Grantham and to Alfred Roberts' shop', and referring to the journalist who was writing about Mr Roberts, Webster concludes 'For Nicholas Wapshott it is not an exaggeration to say that Britain is currently being administered by him'.

Webster continues:

> shifting of attention away from her mother is characteristic of Mrs Thatcher's treatment of her. Beatrice remains a shadowy figure, her qualities seldom named, much less praised, her existence merged into and superseded by the figure of Alfred. ... There is no inheritance claimed from Beatrice, and could scarcely be one, since she is presented as a figure without identity, a part of 'Daddy' without any apparent capacity for independent thought or action.
>
> (Webster, 1990, p. 7)

What made many leaders memorable and even inspirational was an inner need to prove something, very often to themselves. Most memorable leaders were driven by tragic psychological flaws which established their fame or notoriety. Within the transactional analysis paradigm it could be argued that the parent in the adult leader brought out the child in the adult follower. In other words, authoritarian leadership can only be exercised with permission or complicity. 'I hate victims who respect their executioner' said Sartre.

Many of the so-called great leaders were 'great' leaders only in a strictly value-free sense. In an educational context, when we talk about 'good' leaders a moral sense is assumed. 'Good' leaders know how to put the child and the parent in their place. In a school context a good leader knows that your colleagues do not have to live with your parents, and that when you come to work you should leave the child at home. How many leaders, even in educational contexts, have allowed the child-in-the-adult to roam free, indulging temper tantrums, demanding to be the centre of attention, needing to be reassured, or to be verbally (and sometimes even physically) spanked?

On the death of Deng-Xiao Ping virtually every British newspaper ran the famous Deng quote that 'it doesn't matter whether a cat is black or white as long as it catches mice'. In assessments of 'great' leadership, such value-free pragmatism is commonplace. There were many eulogies to Deng, including *The Times* newspaper ('always impressed by power' as one reviewer put it), and ex-premier Edward Heath, who found Deng a very nice man with a tough job to do. The history which we were taught at school and which Tom Paxton so effectively lampooned, nurtured us on models of leadership which forgot to include minor peccadilloes such as mass murder, rape and genocide, says Noam Chomsky, describing how 95% of the population of Latin America were wiped out within a century and a half of Columbus's 'discovery' of America:

> mass genocide on a colossal scale which we celebrate each October when we honour Columbus – a notable mass murderer himself – on Columbus day.
>
> (Chomsky, 1987, p. 121-122)

There is a large degree of consensus in the literature that the immense, or perhaps really rather fragile, egos of the charismatic giants are not what is looked for in educational leadership. Nor, it is agreed, are effective leaders 'selfless' either. For people in positions of power and influence selflessness may be an equally dangerous and self-indulgent excess. Good leaders have grown up.

6. THE PREFERRED STYLE OF LEADERSHIP IS FEMALE

If 'good' educational leaders are grown-ups, in command of self, effective listeners and good followers, then it may not be surprising to find that good leaders are more likely to be female. This is a conclusion reached by so many researchers that is almost passing into orthodoxy. Studies tend to agree (Shakeshaft, 1989; Hall, 1994; Jones, 1990; Eagly et al., 1992) on attributes of female leadership such as being more democratic, less hierarchical, better at dealing with conflict, more concerned for social and emotional development of pupils and more supportive of new teachers and of parents.

Some argue that these behaviours are explained by evolutionary history and cite emerging genetic evidence of biological differences between the sexes. Men, built to be hunters, were physiologically equipped with liberal amounts of testosterone, while women, designed to nurture children, were endowed with a nurturing chemistry set. The fact that the world's great predatory leaders – Attila, Genghis Khan, Hitler, Stalin – were men is, following the logic of this argument, not coincidental and can be explained as much by their chemical drives as by their social and psychological conditioning.

In the language of *The Sunday Times* journalist:

> The bottom line is that men are emotional reptiles – they tend to lash out when upset – whereas women are like monkeys: they sit down and chat about it.
>
> (Connor, *The Sunday Times*, 2 March 1997, p. 6)

While perhaps offensive in equal proportion to both women and men, the statement is derived from neurological evidence on male tendencies to use the reptilian (or limbic) brain when dealing with emotions, while women are more prone to use the primate part of the brain.

This biologically deterministic explanation for gender differences may be used as evidence to either confirm or disprove the nature-nurture controversy. The socialisation of babies, little girls and growing women may be what trains the highly plastic and infinitely impressionable brain to use its emotional intelligence more intelligently. In other words, the feminine qualities of leadership are not only for females. Indeed the evidence for their visibility in female school leadership may be because women have more social permission to exhibit those traits publicly. As Adler and colleagues (1993) suggest, they have more behavioural options open to them and are not seen as violating their gender stereotype if they display warmth and approachability.

If men are, in general, less comfortable in using this feminine side of their personae in public, they may also find it discomfiting to be at the receiving end of such behaviour. An American study by Riehl and Lee (1995) found that in schools with women heads, men teachers tended to rate women leaders less positively than did their female colleagues. The researchers also found that the ways in which men and women assessed power, support and collegiality were also different. Women were more likely than men to rate collegiality highly in schools headed by women. Women teachers and leaders also shared a different relationship with power, mistrusting power in the sense of unilateral domination and being more attracted to the notion of 'power with' rather than 'power over' (Riehl and Lee, 1995, p. 911).

'Effective' leadership may depend on from where it is viewed, or what social and psychological set of preconceptions one brings to it. However, conflicting attitudinal data are the stuff out of which organisational development and effective leadership are born. Hard data, says Mintzberg (1994), have a tendency to drive out soft data, but it is the very ambiguity and intrigue of soft data that pull us into the dialogue from which growth, and ultimately truth, may emerge. In other words, rather than findings on gender differences being used as data for researchers to mull over and debate in academic forums, it can have powerful uses in the learning school. Given a climate of professional development and self-evaluation, the data may be used by staff to confront, to explain and to reflect on their own perceptions. With sensitivity and careful direction this may lead to an extension of opportunities for staff to behave in less gender-stereotyped ways.

In schools, gender is often treated as an invisible factor, or referred to in a self-conscious or jokey way. It is often acknowledged in the structural separation of male and female staffrooms. It requires bold and perspicacious leadership to help staff to recognise and address the underlying tensions which are an inevitable consequence of the social context in which the personal and professional lives of men and women transect. Ignoring this dynamic and treating organisations as gender-neutral has steered researchers towards totally inappropriate and unwarranted conclusions. The famous Hawthorne experiment, for example, which gave us the universally-known 'Hawthorne effect' may have been deeply flawed by its failure to recognise the very different power dynamics operating between experimental and control groups. One of the earliest re-analyses of the Hawthorne study (Acker and Van Houten, 1974) argued that the change observed in the experimental group (which just happened to be all female) could mainly be explained by their responses to their male superiors.

It is ironic that comparatively little research exists on sexuality and power in a school context when these may together constitute the most pervasive element of the hidden curriculum, promoting and constraining so much of the energy that goes into making schools effective.

In the final analysis, identifying the differences between men and women leaders may prove a less fruitful path. What will ultimately be more useful, conclude Riehl and Lee (1995), will be how we extend and enrich current conceptions of leadership so that they lead to more effective leadership and more successful schools:

> a more permanent and appropriate stance is that all educational leaders should be good stewards of gender and should be committed to creating positive school environments that are gender-inclusive, not simply gender-neutral. New conceptualisations of leadership, therefore, should embody the recognition that effective leaders are activists about gender.
>
> (Riehl and Lee, 1995, pp. 873–919)

7. LEADERS ARE BORN TO BE MADE

Overheard on a management/leadership training course:

Participant: 'Surely leadership is a matter of breeding?'

Trainer: 'Well, I'm sorry, I don't have time for breeding. All I have time for is training.'

Breeding is what parents sent their offspring to the English public school for. It was in the public schools that boys learned to be leaders of empires. Breeding was learned and carefully taught. Much of it was learned though the underlife of the school, the institutionalised bullying and fagging which prepared young people brilliantly for the military and imperial decision-making.

Geneticists may never (hopefully) be able to identify a leadership gene but the behaviour of the genes in the crucial months before birth is becoming a subject of increasing fascination to neurologists. The evidence shows just how plastic and full of potential the growing brain is, and how susceptible it is to the environment which shapes it. In its early years of life, the brain makes trillions of connections from neuron to neuron to neuron, a veritable spaghetti junction of infinite possibilities. The more stimulating the environment the more far-reaching the possibilities. Babies seldom touched and deprived of play, for example, develop brains twenty to thirty per cent smaller than normal for their age. On the other hand, rich experiences produce rich brains, further enriched by social relationships which promote a sense of comfort with self, a stability and confidence which allows the ego to reach out beyond the self.

In his recent best seller *Emotional Intelligence*, Goleman (1996) describes the four year-old whose reading of social situations has given her 'a perfect social map of her class', and a level of perceptiveness which will furnish her with the kinds of people skills that pay off in management and leadership. Goleman also describes Mischel's marshmallow test (1996, pp. 81–83), in which four year-olds, given a marshmallow and promised a second if they could hold out for twenty minutes, divided into those who could and could not last the pace. This proved, as Mischel's follow-up study showed, to be a powerful predictor of success later in life. These 'resisters' on graduation from high school were more socially competent, personally effective, self-reliant, confident, more likely to persevere in the face of difficulties and better at taking the initiative than their non-resisting counterparts. None of this is perhaps surprising given what we know about the importance of deferred gratification. Being able to take the long view is a quality of leaders for whom the marshmallow test is a constant challenge.

The groundwork for future leadership may be laid progressively in those early years, and the evidence of biographers lends support to that view. This does not, of course, preclude the late bloomers like Abraham Lincoln, nor the effective leaders who learn their craft late, who mellow into leadership, or who discover the secret ingredients when it is too late to put them to use. Nonetheless, understanding of leadership always brings us back round to the child in the adult.

Howard Gardner (1996) draws on his work in developmental psychology to understand the shaping of significant world leaders. He refers to the powerful basic narratives of childhood which remain indelibly with adults. How they use those stories is, for him, the mark of effective leadership. He distinguishes four different kinds of developmental mindsets – the five year-old mind which deals with black and white issues, and judges in categorical rights and wrongs; the ten year-old mind is 'excessively fair', interested in intention as well as outcome; the fifteen year-old mind 'revels in relativism', ambivalence and scepticism; the discerning twenty-five year-old mind (or mature fifty year-old) synthesises – understands relativism on the one hand, and grasps the need to take a stance on the other.

Grown-ups in positions of leadership may not have grown out of their five year-old thinking, or may, like Jimmy Carter, be locked into, and paralysed by, the fifteen year-old perspective. The successful leader is the one who understands and can simultaneously appeal to the four audiences, a skill which Gardner (1996, p. 45) calls 'personal integration'.

In his book *The Evolving Self* (1993), Csikszentmihalyi suggests a learning sequence which is not a gift of birth, genes or culture but is, in fact, an unlearning of our natural predispositions. It is in a sense a curriculum for leadership. Using a Hindu metaphor, he describes three veils of Maya which have to be successfully cast off in order to have a clearer vision of self, others, worthwhile goals and how to pursue them. The three veils of Maya are the selfish gene, the cloistered culture and the unbridled ego.

Selfish genes are our biological inheritance and they drive us to do things they wish us to do and which are in their interest but not necessarily ours. The American teenager thinks about sex on average every twenty-six seconds but does not give way to these programmed reproductive impulses, due to attempts at social re-programming by parents, peers and teachers. Sex education in school is intended to give information to young people which will help them to understand the nature of the inner drives but more importantly to equip them with the skills to control and direct those drives. Understanding more about how genes go about their work not only increases our awareness but enables us to prevent being manipulated by the chemicals in our brains and bodies and even to exert control over them. The essential texts to help with the casting of the first veil might, therefore, be Robert Sylwester's *A Celebration of Neurons* (1995), Daniel Dennet's *Consciousness Explained* (1991) or Robert Ornstein's *The Roots of the Self* (1993).

The second veil, of culture, is the human system we are born into which constantly strives to cover up alternatives to maintain itself but not always in our interests. Cultures continually require of individuals that they make sacrifices in order to preserve the mythology and integrity of the culture. This happens at the level of the national culture, regional cultures, as well as at community and organisational level. It happens at the level of government, the local council, the church, the club, the school. 'It is dangerous', says Csikszentmihalyi (1993), 'to take too seriously the picture of the world painted by one's culture'. It rests on leadership to help draw back the veil and expose aspects of culture which are rooted in ethnocentrism, jingoism and obscurantism.

A 1940s radio theme tune started with these words, 'When ignorance is bliss it is folly to be wise'. In Chapter 11 of this book, Angus MacDonald argues that bliss is a not uncommon, if somewhat unfortunate, state for school leaders to be in. He proposes a management matrix with two dimensions – the awareness and the knowledge dimensions – from which are derived four quadrants which he labels confidence, anxiety, surprise and bliss. Bliss is being unaware of what you do not know:

If this were a medieval management matrix this quadrant would be clearly marked 'terra incognita' or 'here be monsters' for this is truly unknown territory and monsters do lurk here – the monstrously unlucky, the monstrously unlikely and the monstrously unfair. . . .

(Angus MacDonald, 1998)

The quadrant 'surprise', on the other hand, is one in which implicit or intuitive knowledge is at work, propelling action which not only surprises others but surprises leaders themselves. His simple matrix is but one example of a self-assessment or developmental tool which can be used by school leaders to draw back the second veil.

The third veil is described as the 'illusion of selfhood'. It was born, suggests Csikszentmihalyi, a few thousand years ago when people began to realise that they were thinking. This was to prove to be the most momentous event in the history of the planet. It brought emancipation from the rule of genes and the rule of culture, and with it the gift of personal freedom. In the process, it spun another veil, as thick as the two earlier ones. The ego, left to its own devices, shapes reality to preserve its own image of self. It is constantly on the lookout for anything that threatens the symbols on which it relies – status, titles and possessions.

If 'good' leadership, in the moral as well as the functional sense, includes self-awareness, social sensitivity, emotional security, perspicacity and imagination, then the critical importance of the early years in laying down this infrastructure is now beyond dispute. But without the ability to unlearn and relearn, human beings would be less than human. This developing repertoire of higher order skills can be honed to become powerful tools to extend people's range of choice, to manipulate them, to tell them that they want things they do not want, or to convince them to do things they have no inherent desire to do. 'Good' leaders are keenly aware of the power that they have at their disposal, and try to resist its seductive potency. They identify governing rules which separate manipulation from empowerment and attempt to follow these in their own lives.

8. THE EIGHTH HERESY

'Anyone who wants to be a leader should be locked up' wrote a student in her essay on leadership. There is an intriguing eighth heresy here awaiting further development.

REFERENCES

Acker, J. and Van Houten, D. R. (1974) Differential recruitment and control. The sex structuring of organisation. *Administrative Science Quarterly*, Vol. 19 (2), pp. 152–63.

Adler, S., Laney, J. and Parker, M. (1993) *Managing Women: feminism and power in educational management*. Open University Press, Buckingham.

Adorno, T. W. E., Frenkel-Brunswick, Levinson, D. and Sanford, R. N. (1950) *The Authoritarian Personality*, Harper, New York.

Arygris, C. and Schon, D. (1978) *Organisational Learning: A Theory of Action Perspective*, Addison Wesley, Reading, Mass.

Bandler, R. and Grinder, J. (1979) *Frogs into Princes: Neuro Linguistic Programming*, Real People's Press, Utah.

Bohm, D. (1983) *Wholeness and the Implicate Order*, Ark, New York.

Cave, E. and Wilkinson, C. (1997) in L. Kydd, M. Crawford and C. Riches (eds.) *Professional Development for Educational Management*, Open University Press, Buckingham.

Chomsky, N. (1987) *The Chomsky Reader* (ed.) J. Peck, New York, Pantheon, New York.

Connor, S. (1997) Men and women: minds apart. *The Sunday Times*, 2 March, p. 6.

Covey, S. (1994) *The Seven Habits of Highly Effective People* (Revised edition), Simon and Schuster, New York.

Csikszentmihalyi, M. (1993) *The Evolving Self. A Psychology for the Third Millennium*, HarperCollins, New York.

Dennett, D. C. (1991) *Consciousness Explained*, Penguin, London.

Dürkheim, E. (1898) *L'Année Sociologique*, Vol. 1, Preface.

Eagly, A. H., Karan, S. J. and Johnson, B. T. (1992) Gender and leadership style among school principals: A meta-analysis. *Educational Administration Quarterly*, Vol. 28 (1), pp. 76–102.

Gardner, H. (1996) *Leading Minds: An Anatomy of Leadership*, HarperCollins, London.

Goleman, D. (1996) *Emotional Intelligence*, Bloomsbury, London.Hall, V. (1994) Making it happen: a study of women headteachers of primary and secondary schools in England and Wales. Paper given at the American Educational Research Association Annual Conference, New Orleans, April.

Hampden-Turner, C. and Trompenaars, L. (1993) *The Seven Cultures of Capitalism*, Doubleday, New York.

Hill, N. (1928) *Secrets of Success*, Schuster, New York.

Hopkins, D. (1987) *Improving the Quality of Schooling*, Falmer, Lewes.

Hopkins, D. (1992) Changing school culture through development planning, in S. Riddell and S. Brown (eds.) *School Effectiveness Research: Its Messages for School Improvement*, H.M.S.O., Edinburgh.

Jones, B. K. (1990) The gender difference hypothesis: a synthesis of research findings, *Educational Administration Quarterly*, Vol. 26, pp. 5–37.

Leithwood, K. A. (1992) The move towards transformational leadership, *Educational Leadership*, Vol. 49, no. 5, pp. 8–12.

McBer (1975) *Soft Still Competencies*, McBer, New York.

McGregor, D. (1960) *The Human Side of Management*, McGraw-Hill, New York.

Mead, G. H. (1934) *Mind, Self and Society*, Chicago University Press, Chicago.

Milgram, S. (1965) Some conditions of obedience and disobedience to authority, *Human Relations*, Vol. 18, pp. 57–76.

Mintzberg, H. (1994) *The Rise and Fall of Strategic Planning*, Prentice, New York.

Murphy, J. (1994) Transformational change and the evolving role of the principal, in J. Murphy and K. Seashore Louis (eds.) *Reshaping the Principalship: Insights from Transformational Reform Efforts*, Corwin, Newbury Park.

Nanus, B. (1992) *Visionary Leadership*, Jossey-Bass, San Francisco.

Ornstein, R. (1993) *The Roots of the Self*, Harper Rowe, San Francisco.

Ostrander, S. and Schroeder, L. (1996) *Superlearning 2000*, Dell, New York.

Pinker, S. (1994) *The Language Instinct*, Penguin, London.

Riehl, C. and Lee, V. E. (1995) Gender, Organisation and Leadership, in K. Leithwood et al. (eds.) *International Handbook of Educational Leadership and Administration*, Kluwer, Dordrecht.

Roberts, A. (1994) *Eminent Churchillians*, Weidenfeld and Nicolson, London.

Senge, P. (1990) *The Fifth Discipline: The Art and Practice of the Learning Organisation*, Doubleday, New York.

Shakeshaft, C. (1989) *Women in Educational Administration*, Unwin, Newbury Park.

Svantesson, I. (1996) *Mind Mapping and Memory*, Kogan Page, London.

Sylwester, R. (1995) *A Celebration of Neurons. An Educator's Guide to the Human Brain*, Association for Supervision and Curriculum Development, Alexandria, Virginia.

Webster, W. (1990) *Not a Man to Match Her*, The Women's Press, London.

2

Time for a Change

John MacBeath, Leif Moos, Kathryn Riley

INTRODUCTION

In 1979, Bob Dylan wrote 'the times they are a changing'. Not only are things different as time goes by but time itself is different. The notion that the nature and quality of time itself is changing is one we can grasp easily at an emotional level but find difficult to accept at an intellectual level. Time as measured by the orbit of the earth may have changed little but as measured on earth it seems to have a variable and relative quality. The race against time may be explained by the fact that with each step further towards a global economy time becomes a scarcer and more valuable commodity. Time is money. Its increasing scarcity value and inequality of supply is revealed in the quote from Bernard Berenson:

> I would willingly stand at a street corner, hat in hand, begging passers-by to drop their unused minutes into it.
> (quoted in Lazear, *Meditations of Men Who Do Too Much*, 1996)

Biological evolution is also a race against time. Neurobiologists and neuropsychologists propose that our physiology, which adapted itself over numerous millennia to cope with sabre-tooth tigers, is not evolving at a rapid enough rate to meet the stresses of a plastic environment. Two decades ago Alvin Toffler (1991) wrote about Future Shock, describing it as a collision of the present with the future. For many people the future had come to meet them too fast. He described it as a condition that was going to become a permanent fact of life – that from here on in the only constant in our lives will be change.

The accommodation of change, biologically and psychologically, will be more and more difficult for some people than others so that natural selection in that twenty-first century environment will favour those who not only know how to cope with change but actually thrive on it and are one step ahead of it. The logic of this argument for leadership in any context, but most significantly in an educational context, suggests a natural selection of leaders, requiring people who are change-friendly and change agents. Above all, though, it presupposes leaders with the skills to manage organisations and people in a way that buffers them against, and challenges them with, the imperatives of change.

Toffler was writing at a time when people in education were cautious in their use of the word 'change'. The term 'development' was preferred because it was seen as less threatening to teachers. It implied something continuous and evolutionary whereas change implied discontinuity and revolution. With the new millennium on the doorstep, the language has become more direct and honest. One of the tasks of leadership in the impending millennium will be to help teachers, pupils and parents to come to terms with three major sea changes:

1. the impact of globalisation
2. the transformation of education
3. the new meaning of leadership

THE IMPACT OF GLOBALISATION

'Globalisation' is the word that is used to describe movements that have the power to override national frontiers and cultural identities. It originated three hundred years ago with the Phoenicians' blue-water navigation to set up trading colonies in North Africa, Sicily and Spain. Its twentieth century incarnation is described by The Organisation for Economic Co-operation and Development (OECD, 1995) as 'a widening and deepening of companies' operations across borders to produce and sell goods in more markets'.

The concept of the 'market' is what the French would call 'a false friend', evoking a nostalgic image of a neighbourly face-to-face exchange whereas the reality is the absolute antithesis. Globalisation is typically described as a faceless and bloodless flow of capital to where it wants to go rather than where governments or workers wish it to go (Walsh, 1997 p. 42). Globalisation is driven by forces more powerful than national governments. As Harvard's Rodrik warns socialist, or would-be socialist, administrations, 'financial markets stand ready to pounce an any government perceived to be sacrificing financial prudence to social objectives' (1997, p. 47).

For globalisation read global capitalism. Twenty years ago, capitalism was confined largely to Western Europe, North America and a few other developed countries, accounting for no more than twenty per cent of the world's population. Thirty per cent plus of the rest of the world was under socialist rule. Capitalism has now spread to ninety per cent of the world's population and even the last bastion of socialism, China, has less than twenty per cent of its labour force in state-owned companies (Sachs, 1997, p. 45).

This has brought with it a shift in the balance of economic power. The G8 countries, which accounted for ninety per cent of output of all capitalist countries, now account for only fifty per cent and no longer can act as unilateralist spokespersons for the world capitalist system. The developing countries will account for something like two and a half billion more people over the next thirty years and countries whose ecology is unable to sustain them will experience continuing waves of out-migration.

The collapse of the Berlin Wall, the end of the Cold War and of Communism, and new poverty in many Western countries have eroded many previous distinctions among countries (Albrow, 1994). The distinctive identities of countries with different traditions and cultural histories is becoming harder to perceive. Taking the examples of the UK and Denmark, one can clearly see that however strongly it may resist, the nation state and its agencies of education are losing moral and economic authority to the multinational corporations and transnational trade agreements (George and Miller, 1984). In Denmark, for example, sixty per cent of Acts adopted by Parliament in 1995 were ratifications of European Union Acts.

The movement can be dated back to the 1960s and 1970s when economic and political barriers were going down and new transnational actors emerged and 'made the world their home', as Gasteyger describes it:

Helped by an ever greater mobility and a network of ever more accessible systems of communication the non-state actors became the very symbols of what people today call globalisation.

(Gasteyger, 1996, p. 79)

The number of multinational companies increased between 1970 and 1995 from 7,000 to over 37,000. International financial transactions amounted to a trillion dollars a day, more often than not with little or no control on the part of governments.

In their book *The Seven Cultures of Capitalism*, Hampden-Turner and Trompenaars (1993) describe 'the universal product' – soft drinks, hamburgers, jeans – as symbolic of a culture which has managed to successfully colonise the world with a paradigmatic commodity. They argue that the universal product is, in fact, a way of thinking – about schools, about curriculum, about management. It is exemplified in the search for the effective school, the teacher-proof curriculum, the excellent manager. Many of these have been exported world-wide and have infiltrated the consciousness of policy-makers and politicians, always on the international lookout for the global answer.

Challenges to the nation state have brought a questioning of old certainties: on the notion of a job for life; on the place of organised religion; on gender-roles. The authority basis of many established institutions – including schools – has been challenged. Western European models of Parliamentary democracy have been contested by the emergence of new forms of political groupings and lobbying organisations active in promoting the interests of their members (be they trade union groups, or transnational enterprises).

Marshall McLuhan's (1965) concept of the 'global village' is, like 'the market', a provocative juxtaposition of the comfortable and the discomfiting. Even the media sage, as he was known, did not foresee the emergence of the

Internet, a world-wide learning exchange which allows the instantaneous flow of knowledge world-wide. Ivan Illich's cosy descriptions of 'convivial networks' for learning envisaged these as operating on the small scale of face-to-face communities. For Illich (1971) networks were 'convivial' because there was no mediating authority between learner and sources of learning. It was person-to-person. Neither McLuhan nor Illich could have envisaged conviviality on such a grand scale as a world-wide web allows.

The free accessibility to information on the scale offered by the Internet and interactive technology promotes the flow of both information and disinformation. It promotes knowledge that is anti-educational as well as educational, anti-social as well as to the benefit of society. It offers new opportunities for criminal activity, already operating on a transnational basis from the multi-million dollar electronic movement of money, to the street-level drug exchange, the roots of which reach back into the sophisticated nexus of international drug cartels.

The conviviality of the world-wide web is overshadowed by opportunities for commercial exploitation by those who already control media empires on a global scale. The Third World is already being seen by those with an eye for a business opportunity as one large open market. Support by Coca-Cola for the Nelson Mandela government illustrates how multinationals are able to marry commercial expediency and ideological immunity, and where Coca-Cola led the knowledge industry will follow. It is the simple medium of copper wire, through the main electricity supply, which is able to carry millions of megabytes of information via the simple domestic socket.

This apparent democratisation of information is likely to bring with it, however, increasing disparities among users and between users and producers. If knowledge is power, the ability to use the new media will disenfranchise some groups as much as it will empower others. Commercial advertising and popular culture, with their universal products, have undermined distinctive cultures and are making rapid inroads into national languages. Linguists estimate that a language dies somewhere in the world every two weeks (Geary, 1997). It is estimated that of the six and a half thousand languages spoken in the world, about half are endangered or on the verge of extinction.

It is too easy, however, to portray globalisation as a self-driven demon, like Arthur Clarke's in 2001, beyond the control of its creators. Rather than feigning impotence or using international competitiveness as an excuse, argues Rodrik (1997), internal strategies of training education and social programmes can effectively address the challenges of globalisation. Ultimately, says Rodrik, it is the overall quality of a society's domestic institutions, social and political stability, good governance and the skills of its labour force that will determine where the money goes, not labour costs and taxes.

The implications for education are clearly far reaching, both in terms of new inequalities and new opportunities. The possibilities opened up by the inter-personal, collegial networking of information will have a profound impact on schooling and the twenty-first century will witness a transformation in the nature, process and very meaning of education.

THE TRANSFORMATION OF EDUCATION

Peter Drucker (1993) describes a post-capitalist society which is based on information capitalism. The industries moving into the centre of the economy are those in the business of producing and distributing knowledge rather than goods. By the year 2000, the knowledge industry will, it is estimated, involve something like sixty to eighty per cent of the working population. Economic success will depend on how successfully a country is able to invest in knowledge and how efficiently that investment pays off in productivity of knowledge.

When Ivan Illich was writing two decades ago, he described schools, colleges and universities as the knowledge capitalists, monopolising, packaging and trading on knowledge as an exclusive cartel. In the 1990s, however, the education industry was becoming more widely defined and information was seriously overflowing the capacity of schools to contain it and for it to be delivered by teachers in neatly ordered sequential parcels over a period of years. The breaking down of that monopoly has already begun and will accelerate as learning becomes less school-contained and spills across the boundaries between the schoolplace and the workplace. As Peter Drucker (1993) argues:

> Schooling will no longer be what schools do. It will increasingly be a joint venture in which schools are partners rather than monopolists. In many areas the schools will be only one of the available teaching and learning institutions in competition with other purveyors of learning.
>
> (Drucker, 1993)

The demand for schools to compete in this new marketplace (in which all the ground rules have changed) has regenerated the debate on the purpose of schooling, and its relationship with the labour market. That relationship has for many years been an uneasy one. The minimum school leaving age has been successively raised with the twin purposes of keeping young people out of the labour market and preparing them better for it. Yet the gap between the world of school and the world of work remains, described by Resnick (1987) as a gap between the everyday practical real world of intelligence that is required in work and the formal academic intelligence that is taught in schools. Yale's Professor of Psychology, Robert Sternberg (1996), himself a miserable failure on standardised tests and written off by his teachers, describes 'successful intelligence' as a different entity from the narrow academic version promoted by schools and universities. He laments the quality of thinking among university entrants, their creative intellect pruned after years of convergent thinking.

Speaking at the Seventh International Conference on Thinking Skills,

(1997), the Prime Minister of Singapore, Goh Chok Tong, put it like this:

> What is critical is that we fire in our students a passion for learning, instead of studying for the sake of getting good grades in their examinations. Their knowledge will be fragile, no matter how many A's they get, unless they have the desire and the aptitude to continue discovering new knowledge well after they leave school. It is the capacity to learn that will define excellence in the future not simply what young people achieve in school.

The age-old assumptions about the educated person are becoming less and less relevant to the needs of today's labour market. Teachers represent an increasingly untypical occupational group in enjoying, at least to the end of this century, a job for life and a job in a single place and even a single institution. For the large majority, life is becoming a series of job changes, learning new skills and re-orientating lifestyles. This is what Handy (1995) describes as the 'portfolio' society in which people are defined not by their vocation but by the changing and developing portfolio of skills which they acquire over a lifetime.

The challenge to schools, and to school leaders in particular, goes far deeper than the recasting of what is taught in classrooms and what is valued within the curriculum. It is concerned with a shift from teaching to learning, from a labour-intensive to a capital-intensive organisation and with a much wider definition of who learners are. For nearly a decade in Scotland, secondary schools have opened their doors to adults as well as children, and in some schools as many as three hundred adults now sit alongside young people in the classroom. It was a development impelled as much by economic necessity as educational need, but it helped to reshape the way in which schools are viewed.

It represents a modest in-road into lifelong learning, the goal of which is, in the words of the OECD Education Committee (1990) 'to encourage all individuals to learn actively and continuously throughout their lives' (Rafferty, 1995, p.2). This means addressing a spectrum of individual needs at different stages and levels of learning from adult literacy to leading-edge skills. The OECD argues that it will be realised by an increasing range of flexible and differentiated pathways, through accreditation for prior learning, training credit and transfer. These will offer serious challenges to the front-end sequential system of schooling.

A recent report on social inclusion in the Information Society (1997) published by IBM, describes a paradigm shift away from the print-based culture which, it argues, excluded people by its definitions of, and access to, high status information. The report argued that the traditional system is now past its sell-by date because it:

- treats knowledge as something that can be pinned down
- overemphasises access to information through institutions which control knowledge

- depends heavily on libraries, museums and professional organisations
- allows privileged access to formal structures which organise knowledge
- values formal information and devalues experiential knowledge of ordinary people
- relies on hierarchies and the status of information.

This they contrast with the Information Society:

> The promise of the Information Society, on the other hand, is of an information culture in which informal communication is more valued compared to the formally published or broadcast material in which verbal articulacy is less dominant as a prerequisite for power and influence and on which institutions are less impenetrable.
>
> (IBM 1997, p. 28)

The Information Society raises the status of information at the local community level at the same time as promoting access to information exchange on a global basis. The global village in turn brings changes in the social fabric of communities and families. The changing nature, and in many cases the disappearance of, 'the family' has a profound impact on standards of achievement, which politicians disengenuously attribute to schools despite facing three decades of evidence as to family and non-school effects.

Politicians may urge more rigorous and structured attention to reading, writing and arithmetic in the early years of school but predispositions to learn come from the family, siblings as well as parents. Historically the family provided a mediating social and educational context for children to acquire skills or laid the emotional and motivational groundwork for skills to be acquired at school. There is a growing body of evidence (for example, Feuerstein, 1980) that it is not so much poverty or material circumstances that inhibit school learning but rather the role of the parent or other members of the extended family, in mediating and developing an understanding of the world.

Even in homes without that educational ethos, the nuclear and extended family was able to provide a refuge and a structure, providing emotional continuity and psychological security. There is, of course, a danger in the romanticisation of 'the family'. The greater the evidence on physical and sexual abuse within families, the more we are aware of the lifelong damage that has its roots in the home. This only serves to reinforce the case for education beyond schooling because failure to acquire basic skills is very often not a technical matter but a psychological one, and in many cases counselling proves to be a more effective remedy for a reading block than intensive coaching in decoding skills.

There is an irony in the deification of class teaching methods in Pacific Rim countries when their success is rooted in family learning, collective support and primary education which spends a minority of time on academic skills and a major amount of time on peer socialisation, music, movement, health, self-esteem, laying the emotional infrastructure in school and at home for effective lifetime learning.

In the English language, the emphasis on 'parental involvement' betrays a notion of 'bringing in' parents into the education of their children. The Education Act (England and Wales, 1988) provides evidence of just how deeply that assumption lies in the national psyche:

> It shall be the duty of the parent of every child of compulsory school age to cause him to receive full-time education suitable to his age, ability and aptitude, either by regular attendance at school or otherwise.
>
> (Education Act (England and Wales), 1988, section 76)

The Danish Folkeskole Act of 1975 assumes, in tone and content, a quite different kind of relationship for parents and school and a quite different conception of education:

> The task of the basic school is, in co-operation with parents, to offer possibilities for the pupils to acquire knowledge, skills, working methods and forms of expression which contribute to the all-round development of the individual pupil.
>
> (Folkeskole Act of 1993, article 1.1)

The Danish Act puts the child at the centre and depicts parents as working together with the school in offering opportunities for growth and learning. Acknowledging this has implications for the structure of the curriculum, for styles of learning and teaching, for homework and independent study, for teacher-parent information exchange and for home-school collaboration.

It requires a form of partnership, well expressed in the Danish Act. In the last of those three decades, however, that partnership has been given a political mandate, expressed in two forms. One, the emphasis on parents as consumers; two, the promotion of parents to an advisory and consultative role and as participants in school policy-making. These new aspects of government policy are seen variously as strengthening the unequal parental end of the partnership or as a political kiss of death for genuine collaboration.

Raab (1993) argues that 'so long as partnership remained a matter of good practice rather than legal requirement it stood to veil the inequalities of power under a gauze of good intentions'. He further argues that, in the UK context at least, this movement was driven by 'the government's revulsion against the vertical partnership' of teachers, schools, education authorities and central government, seen as a cosy coalition of professionals and bureaucrats, detrimental to wider industrial and economic interests as well as to the national interest. The establishment of a think tank on social exclusion by the newly-elected Labour government will only succeed, argue its critics, if it is able to marry those more traditional coalitions with more radical alternatives. The coalition among New Labour, schools and Premier League football clubs to run homework and study centres for disaffected young people is one example of such a new partnership.

THE NEW MEANING OF LEADERSHIP

How can school leaders make sense of the changing context and how can they be enabled to respond effectively to the challenge of a new world order? How can school leaders face outwards to a changing world, and inwards to the internal culture of a school struggling to assert continuity, permanence and timeless values? How can conflicting expectations be met, exceeded and challenged?

In the last decade or so, increasing emphasis has been laid on school culture because in a time of change a school's ability to look over the parapet and to deal with change is a reflection of its belief system, attitudes and values. Fullan (1993, p. 21) proposes eight conditions for managing change, one of which is 'connection with the wider environment'. The social system of a school gets to know itself by 'treating the internal and external milieu with equal respect', by welcoming its internal tensions and by making friends with problems. 'Most fundamentally' however, 'learning organisations know that expectations and tensions in the environment contain the seeds of future development.' 'Paradox', 'ambiguity' and 'uncertainty' are new words finding their way into management literature – words which school leaders must help teachers make friends with. They are words which acknowledge but do not describe the external reality. What they do describe is human feelings in response to the speed and complexity of change in the world outside.

Change at the micro-level of classroom level is most likely to take place, say Leithwood et al. (1997), where there is a genuinely collaborative school culture, one in which teachers derive support and stimulation from one another. In such a culture, it is possible to confront perceptions, to admit dissonance and to deal with it positively. When teachers are faced with conflict and ambiguity in a supportive but challenging school culture, concludes Leithwood, they can respond with changes at classroom level.

The culture which supports that kind of growth on the part of teachers is the one in which pupils are most likely to grow and be equipped for the future, says Per Dalin:

> The only way schools will survive the future is to become creative learning organisations. The best way students can learn how to live in the future is to experience the life of the 'learning school'.
>
> (Dalin, 1995, p. 19)

The primary task of leadership is to build the conditions for reflection, open dialogue, mutual respect for ideas and for both professional and institutional growth. In an isolated professional culture, the weight given to management of the individual classroom means that teachers are not challenged to reflect on their basic assumptions and values and are not only less able to cope with change but less able to help their pupils to do so.

'Transformational leadership' is what helps teachers to cross the thresholds of their classrooms. Unlike scientific managerialism with its belief in a right way, and its faith in procedures and hard data to inform decision-making, transformational leadership is about flexibility and pragmatism. It requires the ability to accommodate different demands and expectations. In a time of change the emphasis, says Levine, shifts away from

> total quality management which was largely technically driven, to an emphasis on total quality leadership, which takes the technical side and marries it with the human side.
>
> (Levine and Crom, 1994, p. 29)

Judy Rosener's notion of interactive leadership is an extension and feminisation of this. It lays emphasis on participation and enhancement of self-worth. It is this approach, in her view, which is most likely to meet the demands of the work-force for increased participation, and the demands of the economy for flexible and adaptable organisations. She sees this is as coming more easily to women by virtue of their socialisation:

> While men have had to appear to be competitive, strong, tough, decisive and in control, women have been allowed to be co-operative, emotional, supportive and vulnerable. This may explain why women today are more likely than men to be interactive leaders.
>
> (Rosener, 1990, p. 124)

Interactive leadership, able to respond to the complexities of change, says Rosener, requires a repertoire of management styles. Such a view finds support from a recent study (Riley, Johnson and Rawles, 1995) of women chief executives in English local authorities which found that the women managed across a range of boundaries, adopting different management styles to accommodate particular circumstances. As leaders, the women chief executives characterised themselves as being considerate, empathetic, energising of others but also demanding, pushy and provocative. In decision-making they were strategic and decisive, but also dogged and humble.

A number of writers, Shakeshaft (1989) and Blackmore (1989) for example, have argued for a paradigm shift in conceptions of leadership which start not from a basis of power and control but from the ability to act with others, seeing school leaders at the centre of a group rather than at a hierarchical remove. In Joe Murphy's words:

> Leaders have to lead not from the apex of the pyramid but from the centre of the web of human relationships.
>
> (Murphy, 1994, p. 26)

Interactive leadership may, however, not always work, Rosener (1990) warns. It can lend itself to conflict and criticism. It requires time, and not every member of staff may want to be energised by their 'boss'. Gerald Grace (1995) adds a further caveat. He points out that, in the English context, transformation historically has been the outcome of individual, charismatic and hierarchical leadership and concludes that the idea that transformative leadership could be exercised by a community of leaders rather than by the formal and hierarchical leader would require a significant transformation of consciousness among teachers, parents and pupils.

(Grace, 1995, p. 54)

The diffusion of leadership right through the school is much more likely to be achieved in the less hierarchical climate of the Danish Foleskole, but for them the immediate transformational challenge is to create a collective sense of purpose without undermining the individual sense of ownership with which teachers defend their own classroom territory and professional autonomy. Good schools, says David Hopkins, (1992) are sailed rather than driven. Effective leaders are those who know where they want to go but also know how to tack with the wind.

The school leaders in our study are living with, and trying to resolve, some of those tensions within four cultural and political contexts, historically distinctive but increasingly driven towards one another by the forces of globalisation. From the point of view of the headteachers and deputies who participated in the study, they were able to set their work within a broader context. They had opportunities to engage with the research literature, to visit one another's schools and to explore and explain differences in practice.

As they were quick to point out, however, their teachers 'back home' did not have the benefit of a challenging cross-cultural experience. Indeed, in some ways the visits abroad only served to widen the gap between them and their teaching staff. The effectiveness of their leadership would be tested by their ability to share their vision with their staff and prepare them to meet the challenges of change.

In a situation where the past is all too familiar, the future untried and the present uncertain, a clearly-defined understanding of what makes for effective leadership is of the utmost importance. Learning how to use that understanding to make more effective leaders is essential.

REFERENCES

Albrow, M. (1994) Globalisation: myths and realities. Professorial Inaugural Lecture, The Roehampton Institute, London.

Blackmore, J. (1989) Educational leadership: a feminist critique and reconstruction, in J. Smyth (ed.) *Critical Perspectives on Educational Leadership*, Falmer, London.

Dalin, P. with Rolff, H. G. (1995) *Changing the School Culture*, Cassell, London.

Drucker, P. F. (1993) *Post Capitalist Society*, Butterworth Heinemann, Oxford.

Feuerstein, R., Rand, Y., Hoffman, M. A. and Miller, R. (1980) *Intrumental Enrichment: an intervention programme for cognitive modifiability*, University Park Press, Baltimore.

Fullan, M. (1993) *Change Forces*, Falmer, London.

Gasteyger, C. (1996) *An Ambiguous Power*, Bertelsmann, Gutersloh.

Geary, G. (1997) Has globalisation gone too far? *Time*, July.

George, V. and Miller, S. (eds.) (1994) The Thatcherite Attempt to Square the Circle, in *Social Policy Towards 2000*, Routledge, London.

Goh Chok Tong (1997) Speech delivered at the Seventh International Conference on Thinking Skills, June, Singapore.

Grace, G. (1995) *School Leadership*, Falmer, London.

Hampden-Turner, C. and Trompenaars, F. (1993) *The Seven Cultures of Capitalism*, Doubleday, New York.

Handy, C. (1995) *The Age of Unreason*, Arrow Business Books, London.

Hopkins, D. (1992) Changing culture through development planning, Riddell, S. and Brown, S. (eds.) *School Effectiveness Research: its messages for school improvement*, HMSO, Edinburgh.

Illich, I. (1971) *Deschooling Society*, Harper and Row, New York.

IBM (1997) The Net result. Social inclusion in the Information Society. Report of the Working Party on Social Inclusion.

Lazear, J. (1996) *Meditations of Men Who Do Too Much*, Simon and Schuster, New York.

Leithwood, K., Leonard, L. and Sharratt, S. (1997) Conditions fostering organisational learning in schools. Paper given at the International Congress for School Effectiveness and Improvement, January, Memphis.

Levine, S. R. and Crom, M. A. (1994) *The Leader in You*, Simon and Schuster, New York.

McLuhan, M. (1965) *Understanding Media*, McGraw Hill, London.

Murphy, J. (1994) Transformational change and the evolving role of the principal, in J. Murphy and K. Seashore Louis (eds.) *Reshaping the Principalship: Insights from Transformational Reform Efforts*, Corwin, Newbury Park.

Organisation for Economic Co-operation and Development (OECD) Education Committee (1990) Unpublished report of the meeting, Paris, France.

Organisation for Economic Co-operation and Development (OECD) Centre for Educational Research and Innovation (1995) *Education at a Glance*, OECD, France.

Raab, C. (1993) Parents and schools – what role for education authorities?, in P. Munn (ed.) *Parents and Schools*, Routledge, London.

Resnick, D. (1987) *Education and Learning to Teach*, National Academy Press, Washington DC.

Riley, K. A., Johnson, H. and Rawles, D. (1995) *Managing for Quality in an Uncertain Climate*, Report II, Local Government Management Board, Luton.

Rodrik, A. (1997) Has globalisation gone too far?, *Time*, July, p. 47.

Rosener, J. B. (1990) Ways women lead, *Harvard Business Review*, November/December.

Sachs, J. (1997) Has globalisation gone too far?, *Time*, July, p. 45.

Shakeshaft, C. (1989) *Women in Educational Administration*, Unwin, Newbury Park.

Sternberg, R. J. (1996) *Successful Intelligence. How Practical and Creative Intelligence Determine Success in Life*, Simon and Schuster, New York.

Toffler, A. (1991) *Future Shock*, Pan, London.

Walsh, J. (1997) Has globalisation gone too far?, *Time*, July, p. 42.

3

The School Leader's View

Jenny Reeves, Leif Moos and Joan Forrest

INTRODUCTION

What did it feel like to be a school leader in the mid 1990s? This was the question we put to school leaders and authority representatives at a joint conference held at the very start of the project. It enabled us to begin to identify what school leaders felt was important in their experience and map out some of the territory which we were to explore together over the next two years.

THE PROJECT THEMES

The themes which we explore in this chapter are the leadership themes most consistently identified by school leaders themselves over the life of the two year project. The themes emerging most strongly from headteachers who participated in the study were these:

- a perception of being stretched or fragmented; of having to meet a number of different, often contradictory, expectations; uncertainties for post holders about their professional identity; and what to make of the job;
- an immediate and powerful awareness of change, particularly in terms of relationships with central government, employers and the members of the immediate school community;
- feelings of both excitement and anxiety: some were enjoying a greater sense of power and control but at the same time worrying about surrendering key values and losing their professional integrity in a tide of 'managerialism'.

On the basis of this feedback from headteachers, we went on to conduct more formal individual interviews focusing particularly on what had emerged as key issues for them and what they saw as conflicting expectations.

The questions we set out to explore were:

- what did school leaders think was important in carrying out the role effectively?

- what did they think others expected of them?
- how and why did they come to be school leaders?

We also asked them to record a 'typical' day, giving us detail which would allow us to examine whether their perceptions of their roles matched with their practice.

We complemented this data through interviews with the local authority representatives and with the deputy heads.

The outcomes of the interview analysis and the diaries were fed back to the heads at a series of joint conferences and a range of exercises was used to explore further some of the issues which this feedback raised and to generate more data on some of the topics which emerged.

The heads we were working with were a quite mixed group and it is important to bear in mind a number of possible biases within the sample. Of the twenty-nine who were interviewed, twenty-four were drawn from the UK and most were appointed in the second half of the 1980s. The five Danish heads were all relatively new in post. There were seventeen women in the sample and twelve men. The gender distribution was not even across the three countries with women comparatively over-represented in the Scottish sample.

Within the group there was a significant number of heads with less than four years in post and, at the other end of the scale, six with over ten years' experience.

THE SCHOOL LEADERS' EXPECTATIONS OF THE EFFECTIVE HEADTEACHER

We started by asking the heads to describe how they came into the job, then we asked them about their expectations of themselves and what they thought others expected of them.

Interview transcripts were then analysed to identify all the skills, knowledge, qualities and traits which school leaders thought were important in carrying out their job effectively. These were grouped into categories according to their content and scored across the whole sample. We had seventy-two categories in all, of which twenty-nine were mentioned by thirty per cent or more school leaders.

The twelve most popular categories in order of frequency of mention were:

1 Being able to resolve conflict.
2 Establishing expectations.
3 Upholding standards – showing what you stand for.
4 Being prepared to make yourself available, being accessible.
5 Providing a view of the future, a vision.
6 Courage and the ability to confront difficult issues.
7 Being concerned and able to help people to develop professionally and personally.

8 Being able and prepared to evaluate and make judgements.
9 Being able to handle/manage people well.
10 Being knowledgeable (about what's going on out of school).
11 Being able to delegate.
12 Using resources to achieve objectives. Providing means and backing for what's good.

This is an interesting list in the light of the three themes identified at the initial conference, that is, fragmentation, changing relationships and challenge. The emphasis on clarifying where you stand and dealing with conflict makes sense as a response to feelings of role strain, 'identity' crisis and the conflict situations which accompany rapid change (items one to six). The second half of the list is more concerned with some of the standard functions expected of managers: personnel management, use of resources and administration.

In order to identify what might be shaping the school leaders' perceptions of their role, we needed to take the analysis a stage further. By charting the gender, age, time in post (TIP), school size, school type and nationality of each respondent against the qualities which they had identified, we were able to discern patterns in the data. For instance, certain categories showed a significant difference between the responses of males and females. If one category was particularly favoured by male respondents, it was counted as a response which possibly had a masculine bias. Equally, if a particular category was more heavily subscribed to by one national group when compared to the other two, it was seen as showing a possible national bias.

This analysis produced Table 3.1. Where the word 'Same' appears, it indicates that there was no significant difference in score on the item. The age of the school leader and size of school were not significant for our sample and so are not included as categories.

The two most striking differences were in relation to national and gender differences. Length of time in post also seemed to have some significance and, as far as the UK was concerned, type of school also played a part.

THE INFLUENCE OF NATIONAL CONTEXT

One way of exploring the variations among the three countries is to draw up for each a school leader 'person specification', combining all the categories that were consistently mentioned as important by each country's interviewees. These give us quite crude descriptions but they do indicate how national contexts have a significant influence on leaders' conceptions of their role.

Denmark

The leader should have the ability to resolve conflicts. He or she should be prepared to uphold standards, show what they stand for and wield their authority when necessary. Monitoring and evaluating the work of the school

Table 3.1 The Most Popular Categories – Patterns of Emphasis (Top 12 categories)
(Exp. = Experienced, 3 yrs.+; New = 0–3 yrs. Prim. = Primary; Sec. = Secondary)

Category	Nationality	Gender	Time in Post	School Type
Being able to resolve conflict	Denmark	Same	New	Same
Establishing expectations	England	Same	Exp.	Same
Upholding standards – showing what you stand for	Denmark	Same	New	Same
Being prepared to make yourself available and accessible	England and Scotland	Same	Exp.	Same
Providing a view of the future, a vision	England and Denmark	Same	Same	Same
Courage and the ability to confront	Scotland and Denmark	Same	Same	Same
Being concerned and able to help people develop professionally and personally	Scotland	Female	Same	Same
Being able and prepared to evaluate and make judgements	Denmark	Same	New	Same
Being able to handle/manage people well; personnel management skills.	Scotland and Denmark	Female	Same	Same
Being knowledgeable (what's going on out of school)	Scotland	Male	Same	Sec.
The ability to delegate	Same	Female	Same	Prim.
Using resources to achieve objectives; providing backing for what's good	Same	Female	New	Sec.

will be an important part of the remit and the person will need the courage to confront those who fail to meet required standards. He or she must have a clear vision to guide the future development of the school. They will need good administrative and organisational skills as well as the ability to manage people effectively. They should be prepared to develop a good understanding of the work of the school and be an effective mediator and negotiator.

England

The leader should have the capacity to develop a global and strategic overview of the school and its context and be able to filter and translate information from the outside world to staff. He or she should encourage the development of collegiality and be able to build effective teams. They must establish clear expectations and be prepared to make themselves available to staff, parents and pupils. It is also important that the person should be able to provide personal and professional support for the staff. A clear vision to guide the future development of the school is essential.

Scotland

The leader should establish a safe and happy ethos in the school and encourage staff and pupils by providing positive feedback. He or she must be prepared to make decisions but also know when and how to be flexible. They should have a good knowledge of the curriculum and be able to set an example to others through their teaching. They should have a good knowledge of developments outwith the school and a sound understanding of people. Assisting the staff to develop both personally and professionally is an important part of the remit. The person must be prepared to be accessible to pupils, staff and parents. This means having good administrative and organisational skills and the courage to confront those who fail to meet expected standards. They should be prepared to develop a good understanding of the work of the school and be an effective mediator and negotiator.

All three sets of respondents gave roughly equal weighting to the following:

> Leaders should have a certain presence and be prepared to protect staff from undue pressure. They should be able to use resources effectively to achieve objectives and be able to delegate tasks and responsibilities.

Examining the three different pen portraits illustrates the interplay of cultural/historical factors and political pressures for change. The Danish pen portrait has a rather administrative flavour, reflecting the traditional role of the Folkeskole leader. But it also suggests a need to deal with a fairly combative climate arising from current government initiatives. These seek to change the power balance between the school leader and the collective Teachers' Council which historically has had the major say in determining policy and practice at individual school level.

The English person specification has a rather more managerial flavour with an emphasis on some of the orthodoxies of Total Quality Management. The English heads' concern to keep a clear view of the school in its context, to filter information and deflect pressure from staff, may be a consequence of the strains in the system from central government initiatives. Certainly the English primary heads did seem to feel much more negative about the pace and nature of governmental reforms than their colleagues in Denmark and Scotland.

The Scottish emphasis was on the head as lead professional with teaching and curricular expertise emerging as important. Scottish heads also placed more weight on relationships, seeing mentoring, coaching and the creation of a positive ethos as an important part of their role. The high proportion of women in the Scottish sample might account for the people/developmental focus that appears in the person specification although this may also be due to the importance which has been placed on developing school ethos by the Scottish Office (SOED, 1992).

These national emphases have to be seen alongside the overall ratings of the various items and are obviously not, in themselves, explanatory. They do indicate the importance of context in influencing leadership style and the balance of qualities which a school leader may require in order to operate effectively (Ball, 1987).

The variations may also coincide with the most active faultlines which have developed as a result of the pressure of current reform efforts in the three countries. In Scotland, the main change agenda had been curricular, with devolved school management only being fully implemented in 1996. In England, accountability and the responsibilities of local school management had been part of the head's role since 1992–93 and in Denmark there is an active power struggle resulting from the government's attempt to turn administrators into the kind of 'strong leaders' who figure so largely in the effectiveness literature (Mortimore et al., 1988).

THE INFLUENCE OF GENDER

One of the most significant influences on the way heads construed their role appeared to be in relation to gender. There were clear differences of perception between male and female heads, consistent across national boundaries, although the Danish sample of women was very small. These are compared thus:

Female

- Being concerned and able to help people professionally and personally.
- Being able to handle and manage people well.
- The ability to delegate.
- Using resources to achieve objectives.
- Providing personal and professional support for staff.
- Being knowledgeable about people.
- Being knowledgeable about what's going on in school.
- Encouraging collegiality and co-operation and team building.
- Being able to make decisions.
- Encouraging and providing positive feedback and rewards.

Male

- Being knowledgeable about what's going on outside school.
- Being able to lead by example teaching).
- Being a bit of an actor, having presence, charisma.
- Filtering and translating information from the outside world to staff.
- Knowing how and when to be flexible.
- Having a wider, more strategic view than the rest of the staff.

The contents of the two lists match the findings of a number of other studies which show that there are significant differences in the way men and women conceptualise the leadership role (Evetts, 1994). For instance, there is a clear area of overlap between the key parameters of good leadership identified by women on this project and the five key features of leadership seen as important by a group of American women principals (Regan and Brooks, 1995):

- caring
- collaboration
- courage
- intuition
- vision.

In line with this, it was notable that the women in the group were far more likely to express a vision or view of how their school should develop than were the men.

THE INFLUENCE OF EXPERIENCE

For the purposes of analysis, new school leaders were defined as those who had held a school leader post for three years or less. The rest were counted as experienced heads. There were four new heads in the Danish sample and a further five in the UK. Of the nine new school leaders, three were men and six were women. The gender ratio for the experienced heads was nine men to eleven women.

Again there does appear to be a significant difference, with new school leaders favouring categories at the 'hard' end of leadership style compared to the more experienced heads. This matches with what the school leaders said about the pattern of their career once they became school leaders. The following are some of the differences between new and experienced heads:

Experienced

- Establishing expectations.
- Being prepared to make yourself available to people.
- Being able to lead by example (teaching).
- Encouraging collegiality and co-operation and team building.
- Knowing when and how to be flexible.

New

- Upholding standards and showing what you stand for.
- Being able and prepared to evaluate and make judgements.
- Being a good administrator and organiser.
- Being knowledgeable about what's happening in school.
- Being a bit of an actor, having a presence, charisma.
- Being prepared to wield your authority.

- Being an effective mediator/
  negotiator.
- Being able to resolve conflict.
- Using resources to achieve
  objectives.

THE INFLUENCE OF SECTOR

We did find evidence of a difference in terms of sector within the UK. This was, however, very much biased by the difference in gender ratio of two females to one male in the primary sector and the untypical ratio of one female to one male in the secondary. Bearing in mind this important caveat, there is certainly a more managerial flavour in the secondary list and a slight leaning towards a more 'masculine' style than appears in the primary sample. Again interpreting this is difficult. There is certainly evidence from the literature of a heavy bias in favour of men within the secondary sector and hence, by implication, the selection procedures may be weighted in favour of individuals with a masculine style regardless of gender (Grace, 1995). The following is a comparison of primary and secondary heads:

Primary

- Establishing expectations.
- The ability to delegate.
- Being able to lead by example
  (teaching).
- Being knowledgeable
  (curriculum).
- Being prepared to wield your
  authority.
- Encouraging and providing
  positive feedback and rewards.
- Establishing a safe, happy,
  caring ethos.

Secondary

- Being knowledgeable about
  what's going on outwith the
  school.
- Using resources to achieve
  objectives.
- Being a good administrator and
  organiser.
- Providing personal and
  professional support for staff.
- Being a bit of an actor, having
  presence, charisma.
- Filtering and translating
  information from the outside
  world to staff.
- Being able to make decisions.
- Knowing how and when to be
  flexible.
- Having a wider, global, more
  strategic view than other staff.
- Being an effective
  mediator/negotiator.
- Protecting staff from pressures.

In trying to clarify some of these issues a little further, we undertook to explore the theme of career both in the analyses of the interviews and in further work with the heads at one of the joint conferences.

ROUTES TO HEADSHIP

We have little to say about formal systems of selection and induction because of the nature of our data which consisted of what the school leaders themselves saw as salient. Probably the best way of approaching the discussion which follows is to think of the development of role expectations as part of an on-going process of socialisation (Grace, 1995) taking place over the whole of a school leader's career.

HEROES AND HEROINES, SPONSORS AND MENTORS

18 people	12 women	6 men	2 Danes	6 Scots	10 English

Later, when I began talking about wanting to do some sort of leadership job, she backed me up. I think my headteacher supported me particularly as a woman – there was something she could identify with – and the difference in our ages meant that it amused her to watch my development. She has followed my progress ever since.

(Danish headteacher)

The influence of another school leader or senior colleague on an individual's career was seen as crucial by the majority of our respondents. This was particularly the case in England. Who these model headteachers were largely came about as a matter of chance although a couple of interviewees talked about making their own choices as to heads they wanted to work under. This suggests the road to induction was quite haphazard and would tend to perpetuate and reinforce tradition because upcoming leaders were looking to the previous generation to help define their own role.

The heroes and heroines category was closely linked in the interview transcripts with mentoring and sponsorship. In most cases, the senior staff who were admired by interviewees had also actively supported them in preparing for leadership and in furthering their career. Most of those who mentioned direct support from their own senior managers were women. Local authority inspectors and advisers were also cited as mentors and identified by several respondents as assisting in promoting their career.

For some respondents, an important aspect of the mentoring relationship was the development of 'a philosophy' as to how schools should be. In several instances, interviewees said that they were able to clarify and formulate this through dialogue with a mentor figure. Some respondents also mentioned 'anti-learnings' from leaders who demonstrated how not to do the job. In the case of a number of men in the sample, it was their peers who formed an important reference group for developing ideas.

> The man I worked with on producing teaching materials was a headteacher and became my sparring partner in many things, including becoming clear about ideas and aspirations concerning leadership.
>
> (English headteacher)

This form of induction or succession process was endorsed by education authority personnel. They saw it as an important part of the role of the effective school leader to promote and support the professional development of their staff. Three of them specifically mentioned a requirement to support people who might be seen as having the potential to become headteachers. A couple of the Scottish respondents said one of the criteria they used for judging the quality of a head was how often staff from their school figured in promotion shortlists.

KING AND QUEENMAKERS

15 people	9 women	6 men	3 Danes	2 Scots	10 English

> The advisers were kingmakers. There was an element of political correctness about it, if you were part of that particular coterie the chances were good that you could make it.
>
> (English headteacher)

It was the Danes and the English who were most likely to mention the influence of local authority inspectors, advisers and officers on appointments as an important factor in their promotion. This theme was most marked amongst the English heads.

In their turn, the authority personnel expected to have a role in spotting potential school leaders. It was clear from their evidence that the visibility of the aspiring school leader in the authority was a key criterion for deciding on a candidate's suitability for promotion. Attendance at in-service courses and membership of committees and working parties were some of the things which brought people to their attention. There was also evidence that access to these opportunities to shine had not always been even-handed:

> The education service up here is like a goldfish bowl, everybody knows everybody. There are almost 'familial' connections for some people which go way back. Breaking into that as an outsider can be very difficult.
>
> (Scottish Education Authority representative)

Our authority representatives did feel the climate was changing and that systems were gradually becoming more open and transparent. The majority of representatives from English and Scottish authorities mentioned taking steps to ensure greater equality of opportunity.

KEY POSITIONS

12 people	8 women	4 men	6 Danes	4 Scots	2 English

I trod the usual path in the Folkeskole: chairman of the Teacher's Council the Pupil Council, and so on.

(Danish school leader)

It was very exciting. Working with the Department of Employment brought a whole new set of attitudes and perspectives on how to manage change and what the curriculum ought to be about.

(Scottish headteacher)

Four of the five Danish school leaders mentioned holding office on the Teachers' Council as part of their career path. There is no equivalent body in schools in the UK. The important influence of the Teachers' Councils in the career of school leaders in Denmark might be seen as a conservative influence, particularly by those in government. The Folkeskole Act of 1993 decreed an alteration in the balance of power within the Folkeskole in favour of strengthening the role of school leaders. It limited the powers of the Teachers' Council and required heads to adopt a more managerial stance, so perhaps creating difficulties for some postholders who had been staunch Council members in the past.

Contrary to popular opinion in the UK, moving from an advisory role in an authority to headship of a school did not appear to be that difficult. All the respondents who said they had held an advisory post or a post associated with a particular initiative were women. From their accounts, the experience had often served as a watershed in deciding to apply for promotion to senior management. On the basis of this evidence, the loss of these types of post in the UK with delegation of funding and local government re-organisation may have an adverse effect on the promotion of women.

The small number of heads who were employed to develop particular curricular initiatives also brought a strong curricular flavour to their interviews in comparison to their peers, hinting at the seminal importance of these kinds of experiences for people's perception of their role.

EDUCATION AND TRAINING

6 people	1 woman	5 men	2 Danes	1 Scot	3 English

What really gave things a push in my case was that I took an MA in educational psychology. What we did in the theory of education was very inspiring and led me to question many of the things I had been doing.

(English headteacher)

Several leaders mentioned attendance on a course as having had a significant effect on them. These were not courses in management and leadership but higher degree courses. Most of those who said this were men and, within the UK, three out of the four were secondary heads. By and large the project group did not mention training which related directly to the school leader's role until after their appointment and, in some cases, not even then. Training and education to be a leader was notable by its absence from the interview data with only two secondary heads in the UK saying that they had any management training prior to taking up post. In the UK, most of those appointed after 1987 did list some short management courses prior to appointment on their information form.

WHAT THE EMPLOYERS EXPECTED

Information provided by representatives of the ten local authorities involved in the Project revealed a marked consensus about employers' expectations of school leaders.

In all three countries, the local authority representatives were unanimous about the importance of school leaders being loyal to the authority. School leaders were seen as having a duty to uphold the authority's interests. They were equally clear about the head's responsibility to handle conflict and resolve any difficulties within the school.

This matches with the school leaders' perceptions of what the authority expects of them. Fourteen out of the sample made the point that their authority expected them to run their school effectively and efficiently and 'not to rock the boat'. The sample of Scottish heads appeared to feel particularly strongly that they were simply left 'to get on with it'.

Such expectations can tend to isolate school leaders, making them feel that they are obliged to keep quiet about difficulties they may be experiencing (Southworth, 1995). Given that newly-appointed school leaders have probably had little breadth of opportunity for developing their ideas and skills in relation to school leadership prior to their appointment, this isolation may have left them without sources of informed support at a time when they were particularly liable to make mistakes.

The impression given of the authorities' expectations was that school leaders should be competent managers who fostered good relationships with parents and the community. Creativity and vision were not required. Effective school leaders were efficient plant managers rather than the kind of transformational, charismatic leaders favoured in some of the literature (Peters and Waterman, 1990; Fullan, 1997).

WHY TAKE THE JOB?

Another factor to consider was why school leaders took on the job in the first place. Our group gave a variety of reasons for becoming school leaders.

Power and influence

8 people	4 women	4 men	2 Danes	3 Scots	3 English

> All leaders have some sort of congenital desire to have influence, that is power.
>
> (English headteacher)

Nearly a third of our interviewees expressed a need for power or influence as one of the driving forces behind their career. This was often linked to needing influence in order to promote what they saw as something worthwhile for the school and/or for children. For the majority of these school leaders, power was regarded as a means to an end. Some, however, were prepared to concede that power in itself was desirable and enjoyable.

Beliefs and visions

15 people	11 women	4 men	4 Danes	6 Scots	5 English

Those who articulated a vision of how the school ought to develop expressed a variety of aims. These were driven by beliefs about the needs of children; the nature of the curriculum; the needs of schools as organisations; and commitment to certain moral principles or a responsibility to meet the expectations of parents and the community at large. There was no national trend in terms of what the visions were except that the Danes were much more likely to actually express a vision for the school than were their colleagues in the UK. This may have been because they were relatively new heads but it was surprising that the English group, which placed such a premium on 'strategic vision', were the least likely to actually volunteer one.

While many of the school leaders did have a view of what they wanted their school to be like, this was not always particularly 'visionary' and sometimes quite mundane like 'running the school smoothly' (so that teachers were able to concentrate on improving teaching and learning). Women in our sample were more likely to express a 'vision' for the school than the men.

Just for the sake of it

6 people	1 woman	5 men	1 Dane	2 Scots	3 English

A few school leaders said they became heads because it was expected of them or because they wanted to prove they could do the job. This group largely corresponded with those who did not directly express a view of how a school should be. It can also be seen from the gender breakdown that it applied to well over a third of the men but to less than a tenth of the women.

Women tended to talk about a more tentative approach to promotion. Most said that they realised they could be a school leader when they found themselves in an acting position or after working as a deputy.

So far we have looked at possible influences leading up to appointment but it became clear from our interview data that this was not the end of the story.

HOW A HEADSHIP IS MADE

Because the interviews gave us interesting glimpses into a common set of experiences of becoming a school leader, we asked the heads to draw a timeline of their 'career' in post. They took as their starting point their appointment to their current post and worked through to the present, outlining significant events in their development and pinpointing what had been the 'highs and lows' for them.

The data were analysed, looking for similarities across timelines, pulling together 'typical' entries in relation to feelings, actions, observations and ideas. What emerged as a result appeared to be a fairly consistent developmental pattern.

In all, we identified eight stages in the development of a head's career each of which seemed to mark a qualitative change in the school leader's experience and orientation to practice (Reeves et al., 1997)

The early stages were marked by the school leader trying to come to terms with the school and the school trying to get the measure of the new leader.

Stage 1	The Warm Up	Pre-entry
Stage 2	Entry	0 – 6 months
Stage 3	Digging the Foundations	6 months – 1 year

During the next three stages, the school leader was taking action and making changes. Initially these were relatively 'superficial' changes which served to establish a baseline. Later changes tended to be more substantial and were often more clearly aligned to educational beliefs and values.

Stage 4	Taking Action	9 months – 2 years
Stage 5	Getting above Floor Level	18 months – 3 years
Stage 6	The Crunch	2 years – 5 years

By the last two stages, the school leader and the school had reached a mutually agreeable way of working. Having empowered others to take a more active leadership role within the school, the school leader turned increasingly to the outside world. This was often followed by some loss of interest and a desire for pastures new.

Stage 7	Reaching the Summit	4 years – 10 years
Stage 8	Time for a Change	5 years – 10+ years
		(Reeves et al., 1997)

The overall framework of the stages finds parallels within a number of occupational career models including those concerned with the development of teachers and headteachers (Huberman, 1993; Sikes et al., 1985; Day et al., 1993; Hart and Weindling, 1996).

Of particular interest to us was that this common developmental pattern was seen by school leaders as more than simply a matter of individual development. For them it reflected a process of mutual adaptation and learning on the part of both the head and the school which, if successful, enabled the leader and the establishment to reach a fruitful working relationship.

School leaders who had held two headships presented reinforcing evidence for the validity of this view, describing the same pattern as being repeated in their second headship. Although some of these heads felt progression through the stages was quicker second time around, because they understood better what to expect and how to handle situations, others felt that their second headship had been more difficult. Contextual factors meant that transfer of learning from one situation to another was not necessarily straightforward or helpful. They felt very strongly that the way in which a school leader operated had to be understood in this light. Context was highly significant and the same person, they argued, placed in different contexts acts differently because of different opportunities and constraints (Du Brin, 1995; Ball, 1987).

Common feelings experienced by new headteachers – a sense of both exhilaration and yet tremendous isolation and overload – seemed to bear out Southworth's (1995) contention that the experience of headship in many ways revisits the initial experiences of teaching. Such isolation almost enforces the need for school leaders to establish themselves as strong, independent and dominant. As we have shown, the new heads in all three countries emphasised qualities which tended to underline this imperative.

The feedback from the Danish school leaders casts interesting light on the features of entry to the job. They had not experienced much open resistance initially and they felt this was in part because they were less likely to take immediate action for change than their counterparts in the UK. Intriguingly, they were nearly as likely to identify the departure or the recruitment of particular members of staff as significant, and their comments indicated that conflict over issues of belief and values were just as significant for them as for their UK colleagues.

Generally, the Danish approach to school leadership is rather different from the approach in Scotland and England. Danish leaders do not see themselves as placed under anything like the same amount of pressure as their UK colleagues to be personally accountable for bringing about change in their schools. Danish heads occupy a less dominant position within the Folkeskole than their counterparts in Britain. While new school leaders have their own ideas and values, their task is to identify what the school culture is and to co-operate with teachers and with parents to develop the school collaboratively. The Danes do not expect to have more than one headship during their career and periods of tenure in one school tend to be longer compared with the UK. As a result, the idea of long-lasting, steady relationships is important.

This difference in assumptions and approach raises some interesting issues for headteachers in the UK. How far does the traditional bias (Grace, 1995) towards the strong school leader driven by a personal vision place limits on the mutual adjustment process and its outcomes? Part of the solution to issues of overload is to exhort headteachers to share leadership but there appear to be strong cultural pressures working against this, perhaps exacerbated by current policy developments. It will be interesting to see whether, as Danish heads become more involved in the re-structuring process, they begin to find a change in their pattern of development within the role which more nearly matches the experiences of their colleagues in the UK.

The emphasis in Stages 4 and 5 on relatively 'superficial' and 'immediate' changes matches with the findings of Weindling and Earley (1998) in their study of newly-appointed secondary headteachers in England. There was also a relatively large number of things which could be tackled by the headteacher without requiring others to take much responsibility. In this sense, headteachers tended to remain firmly bounded in the school leader's legitimate and traditional sphere and did not encroach upon the autonomy of class teachers or departments. Allied to these changes, a general tidying up and streamlining of procedures, policies and administration was reported by many of the heads.

The second change effort, Stage 6 – which the school leaders called 'The Crunch' – tackled more substantial issues which had a fundamental impact on the school. The downturn in feelings which marked the beginning of this stage was accounted for in large part by an increase in conflict and resistance after the honeymoon following initial change efforts. Conflicts of educational values and beliefs were more likely to become salient at this stage in contrast to conflicts arising from more personalised issues of style and newness which characterised Stages 4 and 5.

The change effort during Stage 6 was also reported to be more sustained and messy in that it required greater effort and time to attain the desired goals than earlier changes. In terms of bringing about any kind of fundamental alteration in learning and teaching, this stage is crucial. A number of heads never got as far as trying to make this kind of change and had settled for a more limited impact.

This 'career path' has far-reaching implications for fostering effective leadership which is supposed to have a direct effect on learning and teaching.

If that is to be achieved, then patterns of support and professional development need to be consonant with the way the individual develops and adjusts to the school context after his or her appointment. Perhaps if more were done to facilitate building a healthy school/school leader relationship, better results would follow.

During Stages 7 and 8, school leaders in our sample showed a marked switch in interest and concern from an internal focus to one where the external world assumed a greater importance. There was substantially less evidence available in relation to Stage 8 because only a few of the heads felt they had reached this point in their career. Nevertheless, our results match those of other studies and showed that, for a significant number of school leaders, there were some very real problems in maintaining enthusiasm and professional satisfaction (Mortimore et al., 1988).

Clearly different stages place different demands on school leaders. Over their career as a headteacher they need to learn to act appropriately within their developing context. A style which may be effective at one stage of development may become less appropriate at a later stage.

Research by Rosenblum et al. (1994) in America substantiates this kind of change over time as the division of emphasis between experienced and new heads emerged from the interviews. In a study of eight American high schools which had successfully undertaken substantial restructuring, it was reported that in the early stages the principal was often referred to as a visionary, an inspiration and a change agent. At a later stage, because the principals were able to let go, release ownership and cede control to others, they were more likely to be referred to as facilitator, mentor or standard bearer (Rosenblum et al, 1994).

Not only does a school leader need to be able to alter and adapt over time, he or she also needs to have the flexibility and capacity to function across different aspects of the role: as organiser, administrator, co-ordinator, and as inspirer, visionary and thinker. This division of functions is sometimes represented as a distinction between leadership and management. The ability to judge when and how to place the emphasis between the two implies that effective school leadership will always require a capacity for flexibility both in terms of skills and thinking (Dean and Peterson, 1994).

It might also be seen as implying that the school leader needs to be able to share these functions effectively with others in order to meet all the leadership 'requirements' of the school.

SHARING LEADERSHIP

This section largely draws on evidence provided by the deputy school leaders in the UK.

The deputy heads saw themselves as having a definite focus on people rather than administration. Several described themselves as being the person who 'remembers what it's like to be a teacher' and saw their role as acting as a buffer between the staff and the head, 'partly bridge and a filter', as one English deputy described it. They also saw themselves as the ones who 'keep a finger on the pulse' and know what is going on in school.

Many of the deputies in the UK, and all the deputies in Denmark, had a substantial teaching commitment and this in itself set limits on their managerial role. The division of duties between the head and the deputy was quite frequently categorised as the difference between strategic and operational functions.

In general, there was agreement that the buck stops with the head and several said that leadership was not a term they would associate with their own role. Only one English deputy defined leadership as resting collectively with the senior management team. Many drew an analogy between their relationship with the head and a marriage in which they compensated for qualities which the partner lacked, being the one who 'sweeps up afterwards, makes sure things run smoothly' and 'acts as a general dog's body!' Like a marriage, they felt that the relationship with the head needed to be worked at.

The Danish deputies' focus was slightly different. The differences between the school leaders and deputies pointed to a division of labour where the school leader took care of educational and personnel matters and the deputy covered administrative and practical matters. Sometimes he or she was so preoccupied with administration that there was no time for a substantive role in school development.

In reference to parents seeing the deputy, one Danish school leader observed:

> There is also the question of whom parents want to talk to; and of course they want the school leader.
>
> (Danish headteacher)

This very much reflects the attitudes embedded in the UK evidence where the headteacher is very clearly regarded by all concerned as 'the boss'.

There was little evidence in our sample of much sharing of the leadership function with the deputy head and, by implication, the wider senior management team. This was as true of Denmark as of the UK. However, there was evidence in the Danish diaries that when it came to decision-making the Teachers' Council could present a significant challenge to the school leader and in England the relationship between the headteachers and their governing bodies was a similar source of anxiety for some.

In fact, what the deputies had to say emphasises the theme of isolation. Even though it was obvious that in several of the management teams there was a sharing of ideas and debate about issues and strategies, on the whole the school leader remained a figure isolated by dint of carrying the ultimate responsibility for the establishment.

WHAT DO THE SCHOOL LEADERS DO?

At our initial meeting, quite a few heads expressed a feeling of being overwhelmed by administrative tasks which carried them further and further away from concentrating on those things which were important in making for a good school. As one English head put it, after five years of frenetic reform he at last felt he was 'beginning to come up for curricular air'. We wanted to explore whether this was true and school leaders were failing to meet their own expectations through chronic busyness.

We used a fairly detailed diary format as a tool for exploring this side of the equation. Partly this was to serve as a research tool but its other purpose was to provide a basis for discussion amongst the school leaders themselves, helping them to develop their ideas further. Using this format, each headteacher was asked to record a typical working day. We looked at the diaries in a number of ways:

Time usage	Length of time and type of task (analysis of 15 minute periods)
Contacts/object of	Paper/Staff/Children/Parents/Other activity
Content of activity	For instance, if the leader talked to a teacher, was it about an administrative, curricular or personal matter ?
Location	Office, classroom, staff room, playground, out of school etc.
Feelings	Where expressed by the diarist: 'relaxed', 'uptight', 'enjoyment', 'frustration' etc.

We analysed the results in two ways, firstly by looking at who the school leader interacted with and secondly looking at the distribution of time on the basis of the kind of content involved. We defined three broad categories for content which formed part of a continuum, from purely administrative, to administrative with educational implications, to activities which had a purely educational focus. These were defined by working together with the school leaders, identifying and classifying sixty-five different types of task.

When we compare countries, there is rather more of an administrative focus to the work of the Danish when compared with those in the UK. When we go on to look at the nature of the school leaders' contacts with people, we also see a number of other differences between Denmark and the UK. The percentages of time devoted to different types of activity are shown in Table 3.2.

Table 3.2 Percentages of time devoted to different types of activity

Type of Activity	England	Scotland	Denmark
Administrative	22	18	20
Administrative/Educational	35	40	54
Educational	43	42	26

CONTACTS WITH TEACHERS

The Danish school leaders spent thirty-nine per cent of their working hours with teachers whether informally in the staff room, at formal group meetings or as a consequence of having an 'open door' policy. This average covers three school leaders who spent very little time with staff and eight who spent more than fifty per cent of their day with teachers.

The Danish heads spent one and a half times as long as their UK counterparts on administrative/educational tasks such as sickness reports, assignments on INSET, staff welfare interviews, cover/teacher-substitutes, distribution of subjects and lessons and alteration of timetables. On the specific day which they chose to record a great proportion of their time was spent on welfare interviews with teachers. Half of the Danish heads spent between one and three hours in Teacher Council meetings (on average the Danish Teachers' Council, which comprises all the teachers in a school, meets for two to three hours once or twice a month).

When it came to educational tasks, the Danish heads spent more time than their UK counterparts participating in teacher-team meetings, in defining priorities and action plans and conducting professional interviews.

The UK school leaders were more likely to spend time with teachers individually, though many were random or spontaneous contacts. UK heads were less likely than their Danish colleagues to meet with the staff collectively or in small groups.

The differences between Danish school leaders on the one hand and Scottish and English school leaders on the other, point to different styles of leadership. Headteachers in the UK operate in a more hierarchical system than their Danish colleagues. In the Folkeskole, the differential between the school leader and the rest of the staff is less marked both in terms of status and salary (MacBeath et al., 1996). The Danish school leaders were functioning in a flat structure where collective decision-making, through the mechanism of the Teachers' Council, was well established. They therefore had more frequent contact with many or all of the teachers. This use of a democratic structure to determine policies and procedures has never been part of the practice of UK establishments and marks a fundamental difference of approach to school organisation. Additionally, because of the way staffing was organised and deployed in Denmark, the management of personnel issues was much more complicated and time consuming than in the UK.

CONTACTS WITH PUPILS/STUDENTS

Danish school leaders spent ten per cent of their time with pupils (assemblies, walking the corridors, visiting the playground, interviews etc. with individual pupils, sometimes together with parents). No Danish school leader did any teaching.

The English school leaders spent a similar amount of time with students, a significant part of which was teaching. Primary heads did considerably more teaching than the secondary heads. This was even more marked in Scotland where heads spent thirty-four per cent of their time with pupils, most of that in teaching.

Danish and English school leaders complained that they were losing contact with pupils and therefore with the teacher part of their professional identity. For many school leaders, the feeling of being divorced from the core function of the school and their main source of satisfaction was also a source of frustration and guilt.

Scottish headteachers did not have the same complaints but then they had much more frequent contact with pupils through teaching classes. This pattern of activity was compatible with the Scottish school leader person specification which showed that the 'leading professional' style of management still commanded a strong allegiance amongst those in our group.

CONTACTS WITH PARENTS

The Danish school leaders spent four per cent of their time with parents. Most of that consisted of meetings with the whole school board. Some of the time was spent interviewing individual parents about problems with children. The Danish heads very seldom attended parents'-school meetings. This was seen as part of the class teachers' domain. The Danish deputies spent only one per cent of their working hours with parents.

The UK school leaders spent nine per cent of their working hours with parents but there was a big difference between sectors. The primary headteachers spending a similar amount of time with parents as the Danes, but secondary heads spent more than twice as much, often with the Chairman of Governors or the Chairman of the School Board. Some of the headteachers felt that this was because competition was forcing secondaries to take more care over public relations. Changes in governance also meant that developing a good working relationship with the school board members/governors was seen as more significant in the overall day-to-day managing of the UK schools than was the case in Denmark.

Referring back to the person specifications derived from the school leader interviews, both English and Scottish descriptions underline the importance of the heads making themselves available to pupils, staff and parents and, in terms of time spent with pupils and parents, this seems to be borne out in practice.

CONTACTS WITH OUTSIDERS

Contacts with outsiders were often with other users of the school buildings. The Danish school leaders spent five per cent of their hours mainly with colleagues from other schools. None of them recorded any contacts with authority personnel.

The UK school leaders spent fifteen per cent of their time with outsiders, three times as much as Danish school leaders. English heads spent eighteen per cent of their time, a bit more for secondary than primary. The Scottish primary and secondary heads spent a similar amount of time at twelve per cent. Again this could be an indication of the influence of the educational market place. The emphasis in the English person specification on links with the outside world and the importance of developing a strategic overview would imply a greater interaction with outsiders and parental representatives which does seem to be borne out by the evidence from the diaries.

PERSONAL STYLES

So far we have been looking at commonalities across the project group but the group is made up of individuals and their differences one from the other are also significant. For a number of years researchers (Hall et al., 1986) and inspectors in the UK have been concerned about the wide variations in the practice of school leadership. Studies in the US indicate a similar breadth in interpretations of the role (Leithwood et al., 1992). We also found when we examined each individual's diary closely that the apparent 'sameness' of school leaders' practice begins to disappear.

We found that if we compared the content of interactions which are apparently of a similar nature – for instance, one-to-one interactions with a member of staff – we got a quite different impression from different diaries. For example:

Diary 1 (Danish male)
Meeting with a teacher about an experiment involving pupil interviews to be integrated into a project 'How to enjoy school'. Talk to a teacher in playground about final details concerning the theme we shall be running for the next three weeks. A really good topic – well planned. During time spent in the kindergarten class talk to the leader about classes in the coming year and fitting out a new classroom with running water.

Diary 2 (Scottish female)
Speak to school nurse re: her son's accident. Inquired of X's husband. Concerned. P7 teacher requested time off. Shared personal problem. [She] requested purchase from School Fund. Interested in proposal. Pleased with her initiative. Make purchase. Spoke to the peripatetic music teacher who is having to leave. Tried to make her feel better. Appreciation for her help.

In Diary 1, the three examples all centre around the discussion of curricular issues and the conversations all have a developmental focus. Looking at Diary 2, the interactions all show evidence of a very personal concern for people and a knowledge, and acknowledgement, of their individual circumstances.

This school leader seems to be placing a premium on personal and professional support for staff and on fostering relationships.

Equally we can look at the diary entries across a series of activities which are different in terms of content.

Diary 3 (Scottish female)
Assistant headteacher asked to chase up children and finalise arrangements. Deputy to organise all paper work with secretary. Fed back information to the teacher [who agreed she] would monitor the situation and report to me. Teachers [agreed] would keep me informed re results. Set up meeting to discuss [their] forward plans.

Compare this with Diary 4.

Diary 4 (English male)
I'm going to have to sort out Class 6. In future get X and Y to deal with these tasks. Need to follow [this] up in class. This should have been done weeks ago. [Installing software] Never got time. Check results [of talk to dinner ladies]. Must write to parents.

Here again we can see a contrast. With Diary 3 we get a sense of a person with a close eye for detail who makes clear-cut decisions and who likes to ensure that activities are carefully monitored. We also get a feeling that roles and remits and some processes of delegation are probably established. Diary 4 gives us an impression of someone who has to deal with everything himself and lines of delegation are not obvious to the reader.

What we are beginning to get here is a feeling for the particular manager's style, ways in which we think he or she may consistently approach their role.

Heads give indicators to others, to staff, pupils, parents, advisers, governors, as to their preferred or intended style by means of verbal, non-verbal and written communications in face-to-face encounters, informal and formal meetings.

(Evetts, 1994, p. 86)

It is in this sense, in the day-to-day minutiae of school leadership, that the values and beliefs of individual school leaders are often conveyed to others.

Not all our diaries reveal the school leader's style as clearly as those from which we have quoted. Some diaries seem to show a very reactive type of day which is characterised by a series of problems in relation to parents and pupils. In the two most extreme cases of this type of log, both schools are serving areas where there is a high degree of social deprivation. This raises the question of whether we are looking at the influence of an individual style of management or at the particular influence of a certain kind of context. It may be that where the context is particularly demanding, certain aspects of preferred style are overridden by contextual imperatives.

Nevertheless, other outcomes of our study do indicate that the variations in practice that we can identify are not simply accounted for by cultural and contextual influences. Whilst there are some consistent variations among the three national groups (Moos et al., 1996), we can still detect a range of styles within each one of them.

Sources in the literature indicate that there is a connection between thinking and doing in relation to leadership style. Referring to studies of North American elementary school principals, Leithwood cites evidence to show that

> What school leaders do is most directly a consequence of what they think. . . . School leaders have been observed to engage in quite distinct patterns of practice shaped by how they think about their work.
>
> (Leithwood et al., 1992, p. 12)

Similar studies in the UK show the same linkage between leaders' views of their job and their practice (Hall et al., 1986; Southworth, 1995). Returning to the abilities, skills, knowledge, traits and attitudes which each school leader identified as important in the interview (for example 'you need good interpersonal skills' or 'you have to have a desire for influence' or 'I try to act as a model so that people know what I expect of them') we were able to generate lists for each of the school leaders. We then compared each individual's list of important qualities with their diary entries. In a number of instances we found significant matches between what school leaders thought was important and what they did. Table 3.3 shows the examples we have already used mapped against some of those qualities, skills and knowledge which the same person identified as being important in fulfilling the role of school leader.

What is significant here is the apparent connection between a school leader's beliefs and his or her practice. Of course the match between people's expressed beliefs about the role and the evidence of the diaries is not perfect by any means. Often the match lies between the general bias of the qualities and factors the school leader has listed. We also know from other sources that people's espoused theory may be very different from their practice (Argyris and Schon, 1980), and we can probably find evidence of such dissonance between beliefs and practice in our own sample, particularly if we look at individual factors rather than groups of factors.

Nonetheless, it is important to remind ourselves that being a school leader is currently a responsibility assigned to one person and how they attempt to fulfil that responsibility is an individual matter in which they have to draw as best they can on their own beliefs, understanding, experience and abilities.

CONCLUSIONS

What has emerged from our investigation into the perception of effective leadership is a real sense of how contextually embedded this concept is. At the macro level, we can track the influence of various government reforms, the results of a globalisation of ideas, but these are imposed on a matrix which is a complex mix of the personal and the cultural at a variety of levels.

Table 3.3 Diary entries and relevant qualities cited by the diarist in interview

No.	Content of Diary	Listed Qualities etc. from Interview
1	Meeting with a teacher about an experiment involving pupil interviews to be integrated into a project 'How to enjoy school.'	You should know what is happening in class.
	Talk to a teacher in playground about final details concerning the theme we shall be running for the next three weeks. A really good topic – well planned.	You should be a driving force for development.
	During time spent in the kindergarten class, talk to the leader about classes in the coming year and fitting out a new classroom with running water.	You need to be able to sense how things are going [in the school].
2	Speak to school nurse re: her son's accident.	You should be building up relationships with people and helping them to develop.
	Inquired of X's husband. Concerned.	
	Teacher requested time off. Shared personal problem. [She] requested purchase from School Fund. Interested in proposal. Pleased with her initiative. Make purchase.	Staff should feel that they are able to confide in you.
	Spoke to the peripatetic music teacher who is having to leave. Tried to make her feel better. Appreciation for her help.	You should nurture your staff.
3	Assistant headteacher asked to chase up children and finalise arrangements.	You need to establish expectations.
	Deputy to organise all paper work with secretary.	You should build in monitoring and evaluation as integral to what you're doing.
	Fed back information to the teacher who agreed she would monitor the situation and report to me.	You should not accept anything but the best.
	Teachers [agreed they] would keep me informed re: results. Set up meeting to discuss [their] forward plans.	You should take a lead in decision-making.
4	I'm going to have to sort out Class 6.	You need to be able to make the decisions.
	In future get X and Y to deal with these tasks.	
	Need to follow [this] up in class.	You have to work hard.
	This should have been done weeks ago. (Installing software) Never got time.	You have to make sure that things are done.

Leadership is part of a whole culture and tradition as well as being a manifestation of individual beliefs and styles of operation.

We have seen from the data on school leader's expectations that there are several factors which affect what they see as 'a good headteacher'. Some of these are deep-seated cultural influences, those related to nationality and gender and those which are a feature of the historical background. Others are more contemporary and reflect current debates and reforms.

Gender differences are an indication that defining what makes for an effective leader is not a simple matter. How far the expectations of self and others, based upon particular stereotypes, may shape and circumscribe the way in which a particular leader can operate effectively needs to be considered.

Looking at the biographies of heads, both the processes of induction into the role and the expectations of employers were likely to mean that selection favoured those with a fairly conservative approach. No matter which of the three countries we looked at, people seemed to have come into the role with quite a limited set of experiences of different models of leadership and few opportunities to adopt a critical and informed perspective. Induction was frequently a matter of chance, personality and self-motivation (Southworth, 1995). Despite working with a lively group of headteachers who probably represented the better-informed section of their peers, it was striking, particularly during the initial phase of the project, that they were not used to viewing headship from a variety of perspectives (Levin and Riffel, 1997).

The indications of commonalities in the career patterns of heads once in post adds yet another developmental complexity to the concept. Effectiveness at a personal and institutional level is not 'fixed'. In order to improve the effectiveness of school leaders, it may be worth taking into account their particular developmental stage in relation to their school in providing support and professional development opportunities (Hart and Weindling, 1996). The difference in experience in Denmark raises more fundamental questions about the values and beliefs which underpin our conceptions of school leadership in the UK. If we do believe in a more democratic and collaborative approach, then current orthodoxies about leadership development need to be examined very carefully. Our evidence lends support to Ball's position that the role of the head needs to be seen from an interactionist stance:

> Most leadership styles require a greater or lesser degree of mutual alignment between leader and led and, as the process of joint action proceeds, mutual adjustment, compromise and negotiation all play a part in the career of the social relationship.
>
> (Ball, 1987, p. 84)

School leaders need to be able to draw on a repertoire of styles and skills which changes and develops over time and is shaped by context and culture.

To talk about 'the' or 'one' effective leadership style is certainly unrealistic and inherently dangerous. The evidence from our study indicates that the effectiveness of the school leader needs to be defined not only in terms of the qualities of the individual but also in terms of their fitness to a context which itself is subject to continuities as well as change and development both from forces 'within' the school and from those in the wider environment.

Here again we have seen evidence for the strength of influence of history and culture and how this affects and determines some of the structures and procedures in schools which in turn delineate the boundaries in which a leader can legitimately operate. We can also see how reforms may begin to modify behaviour by accentuating certain aspects of the job and downgrading others and where some of the resultant discomfort for school leaders may arise as they feel themselves pulled away from what they regard as effective practice towards new models dictated from the centre.

REFERENCES

Argyris, C. and Schon, D. (1980) in M. Lockett and R. Spear (eds.) *Organisations as Systems*, Open University Press, Milton Keynes.

Ball, S. J. (1987) *The Micro-Politics of the School: Towards a Theory of School Organisation*, Methuen, London.

Day, C. Hall, C., Gammage, P. and Coles, M. (1993) *Leadership and Curriculum in the Primary School*, Paul Chapman, London.

Dean, T. E. and Peterson, K. D. (1994) The Leadership Paradox: Balancing logic and artistry in schools, Jossey-Bass, San Francisco.

Du Brin, A. J. (1995) *Leadership*, Houghton Mifflin, Boston.

Evetts, J. (1994) *Becoming a Secondary Headteacher*, Cassell, London.

Fullan, M. (1997) *What's worth fighting for in the principalship*, Ontario Public Teachers' Federation, Mississauga, Ontario.

Grace, G. (1995) *School Leadership*, Falmer, Lewes.

Hall, V., Mackay, H. and Morgan, C. (1986) *Headteachers at Work*, Open University Press, Milton Keynes.

Hart, A. and Weindling, D. (1996) Developing successful school leaders, in K. Leithwood, J. Chapman, P. Hallinger and A. Hart (eds.) *International Handbook of Educational Leadership and Administration*, Kluwer, Dordrecht.

Huberman, M. (1993) *The Lives of Teachers* trans. J. Neufeld, Cassell, London.

Leithwood, K. A., Begley, P. and Cousins J. (1992) *Developing Expert Leadership for Future Schools*, Falmer, Lewes.

Levin, B. and Riffel, J. A. (1997) *Schools and the Changing World*, Falmer, Lewes.

MacBeath, J., Moos, L. and Riley, K. (1996) Leadership in a changing world, in *International Handbook of Educational Leadership and Administration*, Kluwer, Dordrecht.

Moos, L., Thomassen, J. and Kruchov, K. (1996) Effective school leadership in a time of change, Conference Paper, London, September.

Mortimore, P., Sammons, P., Stoll, L., Lewis, D. and Ecob, E. (1988) *School Matters*, Open Books, Wells.

Peters, T. and Waterman, R. (1982) *In Search of Excellence*, Harper & Row, London.

Regan, H. B. and Brooks, G. H. (1995) *Out of Women's Experience: Creating Relational Leadership*, Corwin, Newbury Park.

Reeves, J., Mahony, P. and Moos, L. (1997) Headship: issues of career, *Teacher Development*, Vol. 1, no. 1, pp. 43–56.

Rosenblum, S., Louis, K. S. and Rossmiller, R. (1994) School leadership and teacher quality of work life, in J. Murphy and K. S. Louis (eds.) *Reshaping the Principalship*, Corwin, Newbury Park.

The Scottish Office Education Department, Audit Unit (1992) *Using Ethos Indicators in Primary School Self-evaluation: Taking Account of the Views of Pupils, Parents and Teachers*, HMSO, Edinburgh.

Sikes, P. J., Measor, L. and Woods, P. (1985) *Teacher Careers Crises and Continuities*, Falmer, Lewes.

Southworth, G. (1995) *Looking into Primary Headship*, David Fulton, London.

Weindling, D. and Earley, P. (1987) *Secondary Headship: The First Years*, NFER-Nelson, Windsor.

4

What Teachers, Parents, Governors and Pupils Want from their Heads

Leif Moos, Pat Mahony and Jenny Reeves

INTRODUCTION

What do parents, governors, teachers and pupils want from their school leaders? At a time when globalisation is blurring distinctions among cultures, what similarities and differences are there in England, Scotland and Denmark? Expectations of headteachers at national and local level may be spelled out in great detail, especially in the UK, yet the everyday expectations of parents, pupils and teachers tend very often to be left to the guesswork of individual heads. These expectations are pivotal in building a vision and direction for the school. It is these expectations that shape the image of the school and, together with its internal culture, provide the cornerstone of the school's identity. They pose the question 'what kind of school is this school going to be?' and more specifically 'what kind of leadership do we want?' This chapter explores the answers from a range of different viewpoints.

WHAT KINDS OF LEADERS?

In order to find answers to these questions we asked teachers, parents, governors and pupils what they expected of their school leaders. Some of the main common themes were:

- school leaders should have a vision for their school. While all groups agreed on that, they saw the vision-building in different ways. The English and Scots wanted a strong hands-on leader who would point others in a clear direction. The Danes wanted their leaders to be more collaborators, discussing and building a vision in concert with teachers.
- no group in any country was in favour of the managerial school leader although the Danes were most forceful in their rejection of managerialism.
- school leaders should have good communication skills and a readiness to listen and be approachable to all parties.
- pupils in all countries were agreed on the importance of headteachers treating them fairly and equally and instilling a sense of order and discipline. The Danes were much less concerned with issues of discipline than their British counterparts.

- teachers, governors and parents in all three countries said the head should encourage and motivate staff to keep up-to-date professionally. While there was an emphasis on leadership as looking ahead and preparing staff for change, there was little emphasis on change management and innovation.
- there was widespread agreement that headteachers' primary commitment was to be in their school, monitoring everyday life. Their role in the community or on the larger national stage was given low priority.

WHAT TEACHERS EXPECT FROM THEIR HEAD

In the second phase of the project, we asked a sample of teachers, school board members, pupils aged seven, ten, fourteen and sixteen and their parents for their views on effective leadership.

We used a questionnaire in which we asked both open-ended and closed questions and we conducted a card-sort exercise to promote discussion. In the card-sort exercise, individuals and groups were asked to rank in order of priority a list of 'competencies' which might be associated with headship and we kept notes on the ensuing discussion.

In the open-ended question, we asked teachers, parents, governors and pupils to name the three most important attributes of a good headteacher. The question generated an enormous number of statements. Although worded in different ways, there was enough common ground to allow us to group these into a limited number of categories.

Three hundred and thirty-two teachers responded to the questionnaire, distributed as follows:
Denmark,   141
England,   135
Scotland,   56.

DIFFERENCES AND SIMILARITIES ON THE OPEN-ENDED QUESTION: WHAT MAKES A GOOD HEADTEACHER?

Data from all three nations revealed interesting similarities and differences. 'Vision' was mentioned in all three countries by teachers but its meaning differed. English and Scottish teachers were more inclined to see it as the head's clarity of direction. It was part of what they meant by 'assertive' or 'strong' leadership, consistent with the role of the headteacher as the linchpin in translating government policy to the micro context of particular schools. Danish teachers understood 'vision' to mean an on-going dialogue between the headteacher and staff, as well as other involved groups, about the future direction of the school. This was consistent with descriptions of the head's desirable characteristics – 'loyal', 'humane', 'engaged' and 'co-operative'. Answers to the question, 'what makes a good headteacher?' are outlined in Table 4.1.

Table 4.1 Responses to the question 'What makes a good headteacher?'
Numbers = 332. Number of times mentioned by teachers in each country.

Denmark		England		Scotland	
Visionary	30	Good organiser/ manager	21	Communication skills	31
Maintain an overview	29	Communication skills	16	Motivates/ inspires	28
Inspire	23	Accessible/ approachable	11	Clear direction/ vision	20
Listen	16	Vision	10	Accessible/ approachable	18
Loyal to staff and pupils	16	Assertive/strong leader	9	Finance/ administration	17
Able to delegate	13	Supports colleagues	6	Empathy/caring	13
Visible to pupils and staff	13	Motivates others	5	Strong leadership	13
Humane	13	Maintains discipline	4	Pedagogical insight	12
Be engaged	12	Manages budget	4	Consistency and fairness	11
Pedagogical insight	10	Delegates	4	Commands respect	11

It is significant that good communication skills were not explicitly mentioned by the Danes. This may be because leadership operates within flatter structures and the head's communication skills are less evident and less important. In the UK, where much more power and responsibility is invested in the head, teachers feel that their ability to follow the head's lead is consequent on it being communicated successfully in the first place.

A strong impression emerges that in the UK there is a greater stress on the need for 'strong leadership' while in Denmark the emphasis is on school leaders maintaining and preserving the school culture through collaborative effort.

Underlying these similarities and differences are distinctive philosophies of public sector management, culture and tradition. In the UK, New Public Management tends to imply strong 'hands-on' leadership. In England, democratic accountability has been replaced by consumer accountability with its emphasis on 'value for money' (Mahony and Hextall, 1997b), and teachers appear to have adjusted their expectations to fit the definitions of bodies such as the Teacher Training Agency (TTA, 1996) whilst still retaining a measure of scepticism about the validity of those definitions.

In Denmark, teachers are more inclined to see leadership as conforming to a traditionally Danish, flat structure and a culture of collaboration and collegiality. New Public Management has not yet developed as in England. In the view of Hofstede (1991), it is a matter of the deep cultural roots in Denmark which are more 'feminine' and a British culture which is more 'masculine' and more inclined towards discipline.

Data from another questionnaire appear to support this interpretation. We asked teachers to choose the definition of leadership closest to, and furthest away from, their own view of an effective leader. Five definitions were suggested.

1. Leadership means having a clear personal vision of what you want to achieve.
2. Good leaders are in the thick of things, working alongside their colleagues. They lead by example.
3. Leadership means respecting teachers' autonomy, protecting them from extraneous demands.
4. Good leaders look ahead, anticipate change and prepare people for it so that it doesn't surprise or disempower them.
5. Good leaders are pragmatic. They are able to grasp the realities of the political and economic context and they are able to negotiate and compromise.

In the English questionnaires, the top-scoring description was that of the strong leader with a personal vision who leads from the front and inspires followers (Definition 1). On the other hand there was a strong opposition to this with twenty-four per cent rating this definition as the worst. The Scottish teachers preferred the head who was 'one of us', who worked alongside teachers and led by example – the 'best teacher' model (Definition 2). The English teachers' first choice was the second choice of Scottish teachers and vice versa.

The Danes looked for a leader who was prescient about the future, helping to empower teachers to deal with the unexpected (Definition 4). As their second choice, Danish teachers chose the 'best teacher' model. The pragmatic, entrepreneurial, political head was least favoured.

Again cultural differences appeared, with the Danes favouring a more enabling democratic model of leadership than either the Scots or the English who appeared to prefer a more autocratic model. Nonetheless there was consensus in the dislike of the managerial entrepreneurial role and in the favouring of the 'best teacher' model.

THE HEAD SHOULD . . .

A further source of cross-referencing was provided by another open-ended question in which teachers were asked to choose and to prioritise five statements from a list of twenty-eight. The twenty-eight statements were drawn from the teacher's own transcripts as well as from the literature. Table 4.2 shows the top five priorities for each country.

There was a cross-country consensus on 'encouraging and motivating staff' as a top priority with 'creating a good atmosphere' also highly rated. 'Budgeting' and 'discipline' were also rated highly by Scottish and English heads but not by the Danes who put them in fifteenth and sixteenth places respectively. Danes and Scots put 'delegation' in the top five, English teachers ranked it in seventh position.

Table 4.2. The top five priorities

Priority	Denmark	England	Scotland
1	Encourage and motivate	Encourage and motivate	Encourage and motivate
2	Good atmosphere	Budget	Discipline
3	Delegation	Discipline	Good atmosphere
4	Accessible	Good atmosphere	Budget
5	Time for professional development	Time for professional development	Delegation

There were other differences. The Danish and English teachers put 'promote the image of the school' bottom whereas the Scottish ranked it in sixth position. While it is not surprising that Danish teachers ranked it low, given the lack of competition between schools in Denmark, the low ranking by English teachers is perhaps surprising in a market-driven context. It is perhaps a reaction to local management of schools and the attendant pressures. English teachers expressed distaste for marketing, as one put it, 'selling the school as though it's a cheap pair of socks on a market stall'. This was accompanied by a view that if the school was serving children well then its 'image' would not need to be promoted.

LOW PRIORITIES

Some statements were ignored by all three groups, even though these statements had been drawn from interview transcripts in which headteachers described the characteristics of their own roles. The statements ignored by teachers were:

• socialise with staff informally
• develop links with the local community
• be involved in national developments
• involve non-teaching staff in school-wide developments
• keep staff informed about school budgeting issues
• defend teachers' jobs at all costs
• find creative ways of getting resources for the school
• spend time with parents both formally and informally.

While we should be cautious about claiming too much for these data, given the very different interpretations of the statements even within English-speaking groups, there was nonetheless a consistent tendency for the Danes to emphasise the human and democratic aspects of relationships more than their Scottish and English counterparts. A more consistent picture emerges between the English and Scottish teachers. They wanted heads who were equally concerned with financial management and staff relations and who took responsibility for creating and maintaining discipline. This was not evident with the Danish teachers perhaps because by tradition this has been the province of the class teacher.

WHAT PARENTS AND BOARD MEMBERS EXPECT FROM THEIR HEAD

The nature of the survey sample

The parental samples were of roughly equivalent size for Denmark and Scotland (250). The overall size of the English sample was half that figure (124). The sample sizes for the boards were Danes 52, English 46 and 34 responses for the Scots. By and large, the results of the survey were very much the same for parents and board members so the discussion points which are raised in this section apply to both groups unless the text indicates otherwise.

The open-ended question invited respondents to name the most important qualities of a good headteacher. Tables 4.3 and 4.4 represent the responses of parents and board members:

Table 4.3 Parents' responses to the open-ended question

Scotland	England	Denmark
Good communication skills. Listens	Good communication skills. Listens	Having a good overview
Good/strong leadership	Good/strong leadership	Co-operative
Effective management skills	Instils and maintains discipline	Being visionary
Accessible and approachable	Accessible and approachable	Good/well qualified teacher
Instils and maintains discipline	Effective management skills	Good leadership
Understanding/empathy with pupils, parents and staff	Encourages and motivates people	Effective management skills
Encourages and motivates people	Understanding/empathy with pupils, parents and staff	Inspiring
Dedication/commitment	Establishes good relationships	Encourages and motivates people

Table 4.4 Board members' responses to the open-ended question

Scotland	England	Denmark
Good/strong leadership	Good communication skills. Listens	Having a good overview
Encourages and motivates people	Effective management skills	Being a visionary
Accessible and approachable	Good/strong leadership	Co-operative
Effective management skills	Gives a clear direction to the school. Vision	Listens
Dedication/commitment	Encourages and motivates people	Good leadership
Good communication skills. Listens	Establishes good relationships	Good/well qualified teacher
Provides a safe, happy environment for learning	Instils and maintains discipline	Inspiring
Commands respect	Able to delegate effectively	Effective management skills

Scottish and English groups do not show any significant variations but patterns of responses again illustrate distinctive Danish perspectives.

In all three countries, the respondents place comparatively little value on the headteacher's role in the wider arena beyond the school. There was little support for items such as 'working in the community', 'promoting the image of the school' or 'taking part in national initiatives'. Given the emphasis on creating an educational market-place, particularly in England, this is perhaps surprising.

Follow-up discussions revealed the Danes are antipathetic to the notion of promoting the image of the school, seen by some groups as almost scandalous. There was a firm rejection of associating a school with a business. The Scots were more dispassionate about promoting the image of the school although there were also suggestions that it was demeaning and smacking of too much competition. The English teachers in our sample did, however, see it as something that heads had to do. These attitudes appear to reflect the pace of development of New Public Management in each of the three countries. The following statements illustrate this:

> Good heads aren't just one thing. It depends on the wider political context and what needs to be done to ensure that important values are maintained. If a school needs to become visible in positive ways then the head needs to put energy into it, for example, like wooing the local press.
>
> (England)

> Board members were uneasy with promoting the image of the school because it sounded superficial to them. It was more important in their view to establish close links with the community.
>
> (Scotland)

Compared with the public policy view in the UK, there was very little emphasis placed by parents and board members on change and change management (TTA, 1996a,b). Being innovative and keeping up with new ideas and developments was only mentioned by a handful of survey respondents in any of the three countries. This contrasted with the evidence from the card-sort where there was a very definite concern on the part of pupils and board members about teachers keeping up-to-date in their professional field. In many of the groups, there was a feeling that teachers and schools were behind the times and that teachers were overly conservative and unaware of new developments. There was quite a strong thread of opinion in nearly all the groups that keeping staff up-to-date and feeding in information about new developments was an important part of the head's job. Linked to this, in the minds of the pupils and board members, was the notion that it is the role of the head to make sure the teachers were 'up-to-scratch'.

> parents found it more important that the leader motivated and encouraged teachers and kept up their theoretical knowledge than that they taught classes.
>
> (Denmark)

You've always got a range of teachers from new to experienced. The new teachers need supporting into a new job and your experienced teachers need to be kept up-to-date. A head's got to give this some importance because things have changed a lot.

The head needs to be up-to-date and keep her finger on the pulse.

(England)

The head has to know what's going on and I would want him to make sure he passes that on. Like professional development – it's to the advantage of the pupils that the teachers know about new methods and the head needs to ensure they're up-to-date. He needs to ensure information is coming in from the outside and the place isn't stagnating.

(Scotland)

All survey respondents saw effective management skills and the ability to motivate and lead people as essential attributes of a headteacher. The responses in relation to the management were fairly undifferentiated except in the area of interpersonal skills where there were several categories consistently identified by respondents: communication, empathy, accessibility, ability to motivate and inspire.

Interestingly there does not appear to be a great deal of difference in relation to the emphasis on management skills across the countries. The introduction of site-based management in England, Scotland and Denmark did not seem to have differentiated parents' expectations of the school leader. Nonetheless, school leaders themselves felt that re-structuring had altered the balance and character of their work. Managing the budget did score higher within the UK than it did in Denmark. This item tended to provoke some quite heated debate during the card-sort exercise. The Scots came across as relatively hostile, seeing budgeting as something that the head should not have to be concerned with, however important. They felt that dealing with a budget got in the way of the head doing their real job. Nor did the Danes see it as important. The English, on the other hand, did seem more inclined to reconcile this aspect of their role, reflecting perhaps the timing of the introduction of devolved school management in the three countries.

Some people didn't think that it [managing the budget] should be very high but all agreed it was a necessary evil.

(Denmark)

For a headteacher this [managing the budget] should come quite low down; children and people should come before money. I'd rather a school had poor resources but a good atmosphere than good resources and a poor atmosphere.

(Scotland)

In the new climate the head has to have his feet in different camps; he's got to know about business as well as education.

(England)

Whilst there was about equal importance attached to managerial skills, there were clear differences in terms of the domain in which they were to be exercised. In the UK, the school leader came across as a more 'public' figure who was expected to take an active and direct role in interaction with pupils and parents whereas in Denmark the school leader seemed to be expected to focus more on leading and working with the teachers.

In the UK, the most essential quality identified in the survey was that of being a good communicator. Over and over again respondents placed a high value on the ability of the head to listen to others. The head was often seen as the final arbiter and adjudicator between different stakeholders, each group seeing him or her as understanding, representing and responding to their interests. The emphasis on consistency and fairness was perhaps an indication of the importance attached to the adjudicator role of the head, particularly in relation to disciplinary matters.

> I think it's more difficult than a commercial job. Education for the last 30 years has been like quicksand. It seems to be moving all the time. It's very difficult because you've got so many potentially conflicting groups which means you've got 3 or 4 roles to play and you've got to balance multiple accountabilities. I don't think it's going to get any easier because I think education's going to change radically in the future.
>
> (Scotland)

Accessibility and approachability, which were also rated highly by UK parents, seem to be integrally related to the role of listener and adjudicator. The top five categories in the Danish list reveal a greater emphasis on more traditional leadership qualities such as providing a vision and inspiring people. The importance of having credibility as a teacher was also listed, perhaps because Danish parents see the main role of the school leader being to influence the teachers. There was also more of an emphasis on collegial qualities in the Danish list than there was in either of the UK lists, with co-operation and the ability to delegate figuring high in the ranking. Neither of these appeared in the UK top priorities. A difference between board members and parents was a tendency for board members to place slightly greater emphasis on leadership functions:

> The teachers think the leader should teach in order to be up-to-date but the parents claim that it is quite unrealistic, and the leader should be like a manager in a company. He has overall responsibility.
>
> (Denmark)

> They should also be steering the ship and that's why they need to know what's going on out there and keep up-to-date with new developments. They need to be able to say, 'We'll take this and that and we'll go about it this way'.
>
> (Scotland)

In discussion, quite a few of the UK board representatives did see the head as being increasingly overwhelmed by administration and moving away from children and their learning as a result. Allied to this was a belief that delegation was being used much more than in the past because of the increasing load of administrative work which schools were having to undertake.

Again, in the card-sort exercise the Danes tended to take a much stronger line on the need for the school leader to have a clear moral stance than did their colleagues in the UK. This was, on occasion, linked to the issue of immigration and establishing a common culture. There was also some debate about morals and values in the discussion with Danish parents and board members, seeing it as a rapidly changing social scene. There were also perceptions that the way in which schools relate to pupils and pupils relate to their schools was changing. There was an awareness of the break-up of the old system of values and the traditional family structure and mention of the contrast between old and young in terms of their experiences.

> As regards clear ethical views, some of the parents argued that this seemed to be an old-fashioned mode of leadership but others said that when you think about all the different values and cultures in the school it is very important that the leader has clear views on ethical questions.
>
> (Denmark)

> A moral stance is more important now. A school's not just about academics, values matter as well because parents don't do it now. I think you've got to watch it though because morals are a personal issue. You mustn't be too judgemental – you've got to take a wider view nowadays and use common sense.

> People's lives have changed so much you've got to be careful. Things that were regarded as immoral aren't any more although you have still got to take a stance when things are unacceptable.
>
> (Scotland)

The emphasis on discipline in the UK responses was clearly related to morality, to the moral authority of the headteacher and to the adjudicator role of the head. This came through clearly in discussions around the card-sort. The Scottish parents and board members seemed to be more 'obsessed' with discipline than either the English or the Danes and they seemed to view it in two ways – as about the control of unacceptable behaviour (teachers and pupils) and as about setting standards for behaviour, social relationships and the social education of pupils. It was tied in as well with establishing a work ethic, being business-like and purposeful.

The emphasis on discipline in the UK as compared with Denmark comes through in Tables 4.5, 4.6 and 4.7 which compare the top five priorities of parents and board members in their countries.

Confirming evidence for this came through the card-sort exercise. Dealing with teachers who were 'not pulling their weight' was consistently included in all three countries. Board members in these countries saw it as important that heads dealt with teachers who were underperforming. The link between

Table 4.5   Top five qualities from the open-ended questions, Denmark

Parents	Board
Create a good atmosphere	Encourage and motivate
Encourage and motivate	Delegate responsibility
Ensure targets are set for each year group	Create a good atmosphere
Deal with teachers not pulling their weight	Deal with teachers not pulling their weight
Delegate responsibility	Keep school board informed

Table 4.6   Top five qualities from the open-ended questions, England

Parents	Board
Maintain effective discipline	Encourage and motivate
Encourage and motivate	Create a good atmosphere
Create a good atmosphere	Manage the budget effectively
Deal with teachers not pulling their weight	Create time for staff development
Ensure targets are set for pupils/keep up to date	

Table 4.7   Top five qualities from the open-ended questions, Scotland

Parents	Board
Maintain effective discipline	Encourage and motivate
Create a good atmosphere	Maintain effective discipline
Encourage and motivate	Create a good atmosphere
Be accessible to pupils	Manage the budget effectively
Deal with teachers not pulling their weight	Deal with teachers not pulling their weight

the discipline of pupils and the under-performance of teachers was made by one Scottish parent:

> It's part of one's upbringing, having discipline and control. Kids need to know where they stand, their boundaries need to be clearly set but it's also about having self-discipline and learning how to behave. The school has a part in social education and that's an important part of learning . . . Dealing with poor teachers is part of discipline and it is vital it is dealt with and not just left.
>
> (Scottish parent)

In fact the Scots and English teachers tended to endorse the view of parents and board members on this issue, but Danish teachers rejected this as the role of the head.

There is an interesting link here with the rejection of teacher autonomy by parents and board members in all three countries. In all three countries, there was broad consensus that teacher autonomy was the worst definition, with English governors being the most emphatic group in this respect. Leaders with clear personal vision and those who prepare people for change were the most popular choices in all three countries. In the UK, respondents favoured the strong leader with the clear personal vision whereas in Denmark the preference was for the rather more democratic leader. The Scots seemed to be the most supportive of strong personal leadership on the part of the head. The following data are all from Scottish board members:

> You've got to be seen as the boss even though other staff deal with a lot of the issues.

> The head is the boss of the establishment and therefore they should deal with the teachers. The head is the person who signals what is and what is not acceptable.

> They give the lead and provide the model. It's not a matter of being liked, it's a matter of being respected.

> (Scotland)

Leading by example and being pragmatic and political attracted neither great support nor great opposition.

The answers to the question as to who else in the school exercises leadership were revealing and showed further evidence of structural and cultural differences between countries. These are shown in Tables 4.8 and 4.9.

The variety of hierarchical roles in UK schools was clearly illustrated in the frequent references to titles such as 'Head of', 'Senior' and 'leader' which were notably missing from the Danish lists where the word 'chair', indicative of a more collaborative form of organisation, kept appearing. There was no equivalent figure in the UK to the Chair of the Teachers' Council, a position

Table 4.8 'Who else in the school exercises leadership?' parents' responses

Scotland	England	Denmark
Guidance teachers	Teachers	Teachers
Teachers	Head of year	Chair of the school board
Senior teachers	Governors/chair of Governors	Chairs of pedagogical board
Assistant Headteachers	Secretaries	Caretakers
Principal teachers	Chair of PTA	School secretaries
Janitors (Caretakers)	Auxiliary	Shop stewards
Nursery staff	Physical education staff	Head of remedial
Auxiliaries		

Table 4.9 'Who else in the school exercises leadership?' board members' responses

Scotland	England	Denmark
Assistant head teachers	Heads of department	Chair of pedagogical board
Heads of department	Chair of governors	Caretaker
Guidance staff	Head of year group	Head of section
Teachers	Teacher governors	Librarian
	Curriculum leader	Shop steward
	SMT	

of leadership which figured quite strongly in Denmark. While in all three systems parents and board members saw ordinary teachers as a source of authority, this was more marked in the Danish system than in the UK's.

School board members did not figure at all in the Scottish and Danish lists but were cited in England, a recognition, perhaps, that the governing body exercises a greater degree of power than the school boards do in the other two countries.

Non-teaching staff also figured significantly in the need for schools to recognise their role in promoting the organisation's aims and shaping how it presents itself to the outside world.

Significant by their absence are pupils. It is an interesting omission and perhaps most surprising in the Danish context where so much emphasis is placed on the democracy of schools. OBESSU, the European organisation of school pupils, has recently published (1995) its Charter in which its Statutes 2.4 and 2.5 define the role of pupils as 'at least equal influence as teachers in the school decision-making process'. In the parallel Australian study (see Chapter 5), the case for pupil leadership is put forcibly by Australian pupils.

WHAT HEADTEACHERS EXPECT OF PARENTS

Two questions were put to parents and board members asking them what they thought the head might expect of them. The top scoring expectations for parents were:

- ensure my child attends school
- meet with the teacher or head if I am worried about my child
- praise my child for his or her achievements.

In this there were few differences across the three countries. Unsurprisingly, all parents focused on matters relating to their own children. The discipline issue was again highlighted in the UK with parents expecting to support the school's code of conduct whereas Danish parents scored lower on this category.

Danish parents also seemed to expect to attend parents' meetings whereas this category was much less well supported in the UK. Scottish parents placed the greatest emphasis on doing homework and Danish parents put greatest emphasis on talking to their children about their progress.

As for the school board, members largely saw their role as one of supporting the work of the school. The supportive role appeared to have a greater significance for board members than did involvement in school development planning although this too was clearly seen as a legitimate and significant part of the role by a majority.

A good working relationship with the school board needs to be in the top ten. You need to have the board behind you because they're your arm into the community. Even if you have better ways of getting advice it still makes sense to think of using the school board. They can keep your feet on the ground.

(Danish headteacher)

The item 'makes suggestions about priorities for the school' was perversely (given the role of English governors) scored more highly in Denmark than in England. Surprisingly too, Scots appeared to be the most 'political' group in that they placed greater emphasis on their role in lobbying and protesting to external authorities than Board members from the other two countries. This suggests one way in which board members may support the work of the school by actively defending it against external imposition.

WHAT PUPILS WANT FROM THEIR HEADS

The views of younger children were gained in two ways. Firstly, pupils were given a simplified questionnaire in which they were asked what they thought a good head was like, what he or she did and how he or she had become a headteacher. They could record their answers either in writing or by drawing pictures and most did both. Their writing was analysed and the incidence of key phrases was recorded and ranked. From a total of over fifty phrases from each country, the top ten are shown in Table 4.10. Later, two focus groups from each school, selected by class teachers, 'volunteered' to talk to members of the research team in greater depth. Mostly, children contributed constructively even though the view was expressed on more than one occasion that 'it's a very funny thing to talk about'. Once, in an attempt to inject some energy into a group whose responses were less than engaged, a member of the team asked what a bad headteacher would be like. Though the strategy was successful in provoking some highly imaginative answers, it is not one to be recommended to those who value order and discipline (or who are sensitive to parental complaint about their children having nightmares).

It became apparent both from the questionnaires and from the focus group discussions that many of the younger children found difficulty in distinguishing between what a headteacher is or does from what a good headteacher is or does. Even when children had grasped this distinction, it was not clear to the budding Aristotelians in the focus groups whether being a good head meant that a person performed the job of being a head well or whether a good head could be a good person but 'get all the things in a muddle'. This said, there would appear to be a number of differences in how younger children from Denmark, England and Scotland define what it is to be a good headteacher.

As can be seen from Table 4.10, 'kind' was rated first for Denmark and Scotland, though only as sixteenth for England. Here we might pause to question why these English children identified the role of the head so much with 'telling children off if they are naughty'. It could be that other adults take a more proactive role in Denmark and Scotland as it seems unlikely that

A headteacher writes letters about discos and she keeps old books. She teaches the children songs and she talks on the telephone

Fig. 4.1 What does a headteacher do?

Table 4.10 Students' responses to questions regarding what a head does and what a good head is like

	Denmark	No. of phrases	England	No. of phrases	Scotland	No. of phrases
1	Kind	29	Tells children off if they're naughty	45	Is nice/kind	59
2	Sympathetic	7	Good organiser	42	Ensures there is no bullying	43
3	Keeps school orderly	7	Helps teacher/ children	25	Sense of humour/ good fun	37
4	Tells children off if they're naughty	7	Buys things for the school	25	Strict/good discipline	36
5	Solves problems	6	Runs the school properly	22	Understanding	32
6	Arranges good outings	6	Sorts out arguments/ problems	21	Helpful	29
7	Happy	6	Friendly to parents	15	Happy/cheerful	24
8	Good to kids	4	Teaches classes	15	Treats children fairly	23
9	Walks the school	4	Praises children	11	Likes children	22
10	Keeps the school clean	2	Makes sure children are OK/safe	11	Listens to what we have to say	21

these children are better behaved. It could be that expectations and interpretations of behaviour are different across the three countries. Some, for instance, might claim that the English expect higher standards of behaviour from children, while others might point to lower levels of understanding and empathy. Both could claim evidence from stereotypes of cultural norms and both would create the context for more telling off.

It is possible that younger children in England are merely expressing the micro effects of the current preoccupation with academic achievement such that even the smallest misdemeanour is construed as disrupting the 'true purposes of schooling' (Mahoney and Hextall, 1997a). One might go further and argue that the need for schools in England to maintain popularity with parents, who otherwise might choose another school, puts pressure on headteachers to be highly visible in maintaining discipline. Such a view would be to ignore a long 'headmaster tradition' in England which:

> although formed in the exclusive contexts of upper-class education in England, can be seen to have had significant cultural and pedagogic mediations in other sectors of English schooling. Its construct of school leadership and its culture of headship as personal, powerful, controlling, moralising and patriarchal has

become an important constituent in the subsequent discourse and practice of school headship.

(Grace, 1995, p. 11)

Some of the differences among the groups are worth noting. Only Danish and Scottish children rated within the top ten key phrases 'understanding' and 'walks (or is around) the school'. Only English and Scottish children rated 'strict' and only Danish and English children prioritised 'tells children off if they're naughty'. However, these did appear in all the full lists.

Indicative of the difference between England and Scotland and the extent to which the financial management of schools has been devolved, is the comment from Scotland that the mark of the good head is someone who 'does fund-raising for charity'. In England, many schools also undertake fund-raising, but for themselves.

At the other end of the scale are real glimpses of headship from the child's point of view. In Denmark a good head 'accepts complaints', 'pays attention to unhappy kids', 'doesn't use the rod' and 'makes an aerial ropeway'. In England he or she 'talks about the good news', 'cheers you up' and 'protects education'. In Scotland, he or she 'keeps the playground tidy', 'has music/sporting skills' and 'is good with bad children, for example, keeping them in at playtime and posting letters to parents of very bad children'.

The good headteacher's responsibilities are heavy indeed and all heads would do well to remember the dire consequences, as described by this Danish boy, of not anticipating what can go wrong:

> To me a good headteacher is good at solving problems. They should not agree to spending money for anything stupid. They should not just sit on their behind and do nothing about complaints like if my big brother attended this school and was being pestered by someone. He hit him but he moved so my big brother hit a window. Then the headteacher came and got hold of him and got blood on his shirt and my big brother was expelled.

(Danish pupil)

OLDER STUDENTS

Table 4.11 shows the top ten statements using the pupils' own words in answer to the question 'What is a good headteacher?'

As can be seen from Table 4.11, beneath the superficial differences in expression, there was a large measure of agreement among the older pupils from all three countries. If the statements 'listens', 'talks with pupils', 'nice/kind to pupils', 'takes care of pupils', 'understands pupils', 'establishes good relationships', 'sense of humour' and 'accessible/approachable' are taken together and interpreted as falling under a broader category of 'establishing positive relationships', then the data are overwhelming that, for older students, this is the most important criterion of good headship.

Similarly if 'fair' and 'treats pupils equally' are taken together with a

Table 4.11 Older pupils' responses to the question 'what is a good headteacher?'

	Denmark	No. of phrases	England	No. of phrases	Scotland	No. of phrases
1	Listens	37	Fair	16	Listens	67
2	Talks with pupils	36	Good relationships with pupils/teachers	9	Is understanding	55
3	Kind	30	Accessible/ approachable	7	Treats children fairly	46
4	Nice to pupils	29	Caring	7	Strict/ good discipline	45
5	Treats pupils equally	24	Understands pupils	7	Someone to talk to/talks to us	45
6	Keeps school nice, clean/orderly	23	Takes account of pupils' opinions	6	Good relationships with pupils	44
7	Takes care of pupils	19	Good listener	6	Sense of humour/ good fun	35
8	Manages the school	16	Responsible	5	Looks after/capable of running school	27
9	Respectable	15	Treats people equally	5	Is nice/kind	24
10	Understands pupils	14	Maintains discipline	4	Not too strict	21

concern that headteachers should be just in their dealings with pupils, then again there is a wide measure of agreement. This interpretation can be justified on the grounds that in another part of the questionnaire they gave top marks to the statement 'treat pupils fairly'.

The issue of meaning (with which we have constantly struggled throughout the project), re-emerges in relation to what Danish students mean by 'respectable'. Do they really mean 'of fair social standing; honest and decent in conduct' *(Concise Oxford Dictionary)*? If they do, this would fly in the face of other evidence from headteachers, including our own:

> In a survey of 1,000 school headteachers . . . the respondents identified one of the most important characteristics of the successful school headteacher to be 'A healthy disrespect of authority'. This implied a deviousness needed in management to circumvent the constraining formal systems of control.
>
> (Boyett and Finlay, 1996, p. 33)

Alternatively, do they mean 'deserving of respect'? If the latter, then again there would be little disagreement from their English counterparts about the overall importance of respect, though who should respect whom is stated in reverse. For the English pupils, the need for the head to 'respect others' was placed within the top fifteen statements whereas for Danish pupils 'respects pupils' is well down the list at forty-fourth.

Maybe this discussion is made clear when one reads the following statement made by one secondary Scottish pupil during a card-sort exercise:

Teachers should set a good example to all their pupils and the head should make sure they do because it's his school and everybody looks up to him or her. They are the people who draw the line.

(Scottish pupil)

Although the Danish pupils do not mention 'discipline' within the top ten (it comes eighty-second in the Danish list), they do prioritise that element of the head's role which related to maintaining an 'orderly' school. However, in another part of the questionnaire they were asked to indicate the level of importance they attached to a number of activities which heads might undertake. Whereas English and Scottish pupils both ranked highly the statement 'makes sure there is good behaviour in the school', it appeared way down the list for the Danes. This raises interesting questions about cultural differences in how 'discipline' is conceptualised and who is viewed as having responsibility for its maintenance in Denmark. It seems to be part of the Danish school culture to allocate the responsibility for upholding a good discipline to the class teacher. He or she often follows the class for several years (for up to nine years) and is the main link to parents.

Though one Scottish pupil felt that the good head is 'someone who is strict when needs to be but righteous in his judicial decisions', overall for this group 'not too strict' appears within the top ten. On the other hand, 'strict' is ranked twelfth for the English. There may be a cultural factor here with English pupils having been bombarded of late with a tabloid press which constantly bemoans England's rampaging youth (while inciting them), the decline of the nation's moral fibre in general and child-centred teaching methods in particular. 'Strict' does not figure in any shape or form for the Danes in any one of the one hundred and forty-six statements.

Equally interesting is what else the pupils said which did not enter the top ten. Older pupils from all three countries wanted heads to be involved in the school, not just visible. In fact visibility, which was such a strong element of the headteacher interviews, figured hardly at all, though again this might simply be a matter of language use. The good head also visits classes. Pupils seemed not to share the concern, expressed by Danish heads, that visiting classes might well be construed as 'spying on colleagues'. On the contrary, a significant number of Danish pupils, believed that a good head ensures that 'teachers are teaching well'.

A minority of Scottish and Danish pupils believed that a good head is not sexist or racist whereas this was not mentioned at all by English pupils, a little surprising given the emphasis on 'Equal Opportunities' in the 1980s. Only one response across all three countries openly stated that a good head is 'a man', indicating that some pupils have less stereotyped views than some governing bodies in our sample. On the other hand, this pupil clearly had a man in mind when he or she mentioned 'a figurehead to gallantly lead his pupils into the challenges which lie ahead'.

The subject of the good head's age emerges at the lower end of the Scottish list and at twenty-ninth in the Danish list. English pupils did not mention it at all. Heads should not be older than '50, 40, 30' according to the Danish pupils (clearly what counts as being old is a matter of some dispute) and for the Scottish pupils, good heads are 'reasonably young' or 'not too old so they can remember what it was like to be a kid and like surfing and gossiping'.

Given that there is a greater degree of financial local management of schools in England, it is surprising that older English pupils do not mention this aspect of the head's role at all. For them the emphasis is almost entirely on the quality of relationships he or she ought to establish and what personal qualities a good head should have. He or she should be 'human (not like a robot)' for example, 'friendly', 'motivate others' and 'support pupil/teacher relationships'. These are also important for Danish and Scottish pupils but in addition, being 'financially knowledgeable' (Danish pupils) or 'good with money' (Scottish) also figures. Other aspects important for Scottish pupils are 'someone you can trust'; 'ensures there's no bullying'; 'self controlled/good tempered and doesn't shout at you'; 'happy/cheerful'; 'knowledgeable/intelligent'; 'knows the pupils' and 'is loyal to pupils/staff'. For the Danes, 'lively', 'resolute', 'devoted to work', 'creative' and 'not old fashioned' all commanded a fair measure of support in addition to the comments from the other two countries.

REFERENCES

Boylett, I., and Finlay, D. (1996) Corporate governance and the school headteacher, *Public Money and Management* April–June, pp. 31–38.

Grace, G. (1995) *School Leadership*, Falmer, London.

Hofstede, G. (1991) *Cultures and Organisations*, HarperCollins, London.

Mahony, P. and Hextall, I. (1997a) Effective teachers for effective schools, in R. Slee, S. Tomlinson and G. Weiner (eds.) *Effective for Whom?*, Falmer, London.

Mahony, P. and Hextall, I. (1997b) Problems of accountability in reinvented government: a case study of the Teacher Training Agency, *Journal of Education Policy*, Vol. 12, no. 4, pp. 267–278.

Organising Bureau of European School Students Union (1995) *All Rights Included! European Students Rights Charter*, European School Students Information Centre, Amsterdam.

Teacher Training Agency (1996a) *Consultation Paper on Training for Serving Headteachers*, Teacher Training Agency, London.

Teacher Training Agency (1996b) *National Professional Qualifications for Headship: Report on the Outcomes of Consultation*, HMSO, London.

5

Expectations of School Leaders:
An Australian Picture

Neil Dempster and Lloyd Logan

INTRODUCTION

This chapter presents selected results of a parallel study of expectations of school leadership in twelve schools in Queensland, Australia. It does so against a backdrop of economic and political circumstances which bear great similarity to those which have influenced education policy in England, Scotland, Denmark and other western economies in recent years. Rightist post-welfarist policies have had political primacy in Australia, irrespective of the party platform of the government in power, whilst rationalist, free-market policies have held economic sway, again irrespective of changes in government (Yeatman, 1993). Differences in policy from government to government have been in degree not in kind (Smyth, 1996). It was in this context that the Australian study was conducted.

To present and discuss the results, the chapter is arranged in four parts. Part one sets the scene by describing some of the effects of 'new public sector management' on schooling and on school principals in Australia. Part two analyses data from the study of expectations that students, parents and teachers have of principals. Part three discusses data on expectations of policy makers and those external to the school, exploring how these are viewed by principals and others closer to the daily life of schools. The final part of the chapter draws the discussion together with a summary of key learning from the research as it applies in the Australian context.

1. NEW PUBLIC SECTOR MANAGEMENT IN AUSTRALIA

In Australia over the past fifteen years, federal and state (or territory) governments have been wrestling with the issue of the privatisation of public sector services. The outcome of this ongoing debate has been an inexorable move towards a purchaser-provider model of public service provision throughout Australia. Indeed, privatisation of government services is almost an automatic corollary of changes in the way governments operate and the effects are being felt in all Australian States and Territories.

The Hilmer Report (1995) is the most significant of recent national reports on competition policy. This report, and State clones such as the Report of the Queensland Commissioner of Audit (1996), advocate principles which have become the hallmarks of international reform in the public sector such as:

- as a general rule, efficiency will be maximised by limiting government's role in public service provision to that of purchaser on behalf of the community
- wherever possible, choice of service level and quality should be exercised by members of the community themselves
- government should clearly separate and distinguish its role as purchaser from its role as provider
- government should only provide funding against outputs or results, not inputs
- the management process at every level should account for all resources used in producing each service output
- there is a critical need to impose the strongest feasible framework of competition and accountability in both private enterprise delivery and in delivery provided by government agencies.

In summary, governments in Australia are setting policies so that public services are outcome-oriented, consumers are afforded maximum choice, agency costs are minimised, competition in the delivery of services is mandated and accountability for the quality of services provided is government and consumer controlled.

Achieving these changes has required structural reform in government and public service; allegiance to the concept of competitive neutrality on the 'level playing field' of economic activity; and competitive tendering for the provision of services by private enterprise companies and government agencies.

THE RESTRUCTURING OF SCHOOL EDUCATION IN AUSTRALIA

The influence of the change from government engagement in public service to government management of the public sector has had a direct and immediate impact on schools in all Australian States and Territories (Dymock, 1996; Townsend, 1996). It is now possible to distinguish a number of clear trends in school restructuring across the country:

- moves to school-based management placing responsibility and accountability for the provision of services at the point of delivery
- consumer control through policy-making councils comprising parents and other stakeholders
- the adoption of block funding
- expanding the management powers of the principal
- decentralisation of responsibility to schools for the control of staff, premises, and ancillary and support service

- increasing use of student performance testing as a means for comparing the effectiveness of schools
- the trend to contract budgeting for school services such as student transport, building, refurbishment, asset maintenance, resource provision and school cleaning
- allowing schools to carry over budget surpluses from one financial year to the next
- requirements on schools to report annually to their communities against the goals of their development plans and indicators set by the system
- a 'user pays' approach to teacher professional development
- intensifying of the competitive climate between public and private schools and the creation of competition among schools in the public sector.

The final point is a very telling one. Since the early 1970s in Australia, schools have been funded on a needs-based formula. This has been supported by the main political parties. However, since 1977 there has been a continuing movement of enrolments from the government to the non-government sector (Marginson, 1997). This movement has been attributed to a perception by the public that there is a higher quality of education and better discipline in non-government schools, together with increasing concerns about poorer quality in government schools. Currently, approximately thirty per cent of children attend Catholic and Independent schools.

Leaders of government schools are beginning to describe their non-government counterparts as direct competitors and the search for a competitive edge (Peach, 1997b) is now openly being advocated for government schools. These developments have been given further impetus by new Commonwealth Government legislation. Now, when a student moves from a government school to a non-government one, some of the per-capita funding which State and Territory Governments once received for that student is lost.

The climate in which schools are now working is quite different from that of the 1970s and 1980s. Accountability is now both local and systemic. Competition is a fact of life and pressures for improved performance by all in the system have been increased (Logan et al., 1996). No one has been as dramatically affected as the school principal. Their role has changed significantly, in large part due to the changing role of consumers and other stakeholders in school governance. This change from the traditional role of principal has brought new pressures on management and placed the power of the school principal under scrutiny, calling for knowledge and skills not previously expected of them. This pressure on school leaders emerges strongly in research literature on restructuring. Angus (1992), for example, suggests that one of the constant tensions for schools during a period of restructuring has to do with the limits of school autonomy. He notes the problematic relationship among principals, their employing authorities, the local school council and the community. Dymock (1996) paints a picture of almost daily difficulty in decision-making.

The effects of restructuring in Australian education illustrate just how important expectations are when the network of stakeholders is expanding, bringing with them changing expectations of what school principals should be doing in leading and managing schools. Governments and system authorities are now expecting principals to exhibit the same kind of micro-political skills that typify relationships between boards of directors and chief executive officers. They expect practical knowledge of change management, entrepreneurialism in resource acquisition and commercial standards in school accountancy. They are insisting on comprehensive public reporting of student and school achievement. They want innovation and change in the management and use of information technology and in approaches to teaching and learning.

All this is being pursued in a mixed mode of deregulation and regulation. On the one hand, structural decentralisation deregulates the school from bureaucratic control; on the other, central accountability measures enforce uniformity by requiring the school to meet government regulations. It is clear from these developments that principals are under pressure from policy-makers and senior administrators at the same time as they are trying to work within their own school to cater to the needs and expectations of students, staff and parents. The conundrum for principals is how to meet the legal obligation to follow the priorities of their employing authorities while responding to local expectations. The results of the Australian study throw some light on this conundrum.

2.   THE AUSTRALIAN STUDY

The Australian study was concerned with investigating how the work of principals is shaped by the expectations of stakeholders both within and beyond their schools. We were particularly interested in developing our understanding of the expectations held of principals by those closest to them, namely teachers, parents and students. We also wanted our enquiry to help us understand the effects of these expectations on school principals and to identify which expectations exerted most influence on their leadership behaviour and why.

Design and methods

The design of the study rested on a collaborative approach, working together with participating school principals as co-researchers in framing the project. A variety of quantitative and qualitative data gathering techniques was used including:

- structured group discussion with twelve school principals to ascertain their views of contemporary school leadership, the expectations they perceive people have of them and expectations they have of themselves

- individual interviews with the twelve principals to identify significant expectations influencing action
- a survey of students (584 in total), parents and teachers (272) to extend the interview data, and follow up on any trends or emphases evident through interviews
- focus group discussions with other stakeholders with interests in school principalship, including educational policy-makers, district or regional education officials, school councillors or governors, parent association members, politicians and particular members of the public.

Discussion of selected results

In keeping with the presentation of the findings from English, Scottish and Danish studies, we have organised this discussion around expectations of students, teachers and parents.

EXPECTATIONS OF STUDENTS

Five sets of expectations about principalship emerged from our student data. These were:

- sharing leadership with staff and students
- keeping in touch with students
- caring for and respecting students
- disciplining disruptive students
- treating students equally.

A very brief taste of data from each theme is presented in turn.

Sharing leadership with staff and students

Sharing school leadership was by far the most dominant theme in the student data. Students perceived a lack of leadership opportunities for members of the school community other than the principal. Students thought that the responsibility of leadership should be extended to include staff, parents and, more often, students. Indeed, most student responses advocated participation of students in school leadership irrespective of age. Their tone ranges from rational suggestion to direct demand. Three examples illustrate the point.

> Quite often the leadership of schools is determined by teachers, with minimum input from students. This needs to be changed so that the students have a lot more say.

> I think that a strong leadership team consists of student leaders, teachers, Deputy Principal and parents.

Generally I think that leadership in schools is concentrated too highly in the people high in the hierarchy of schools. I think that leadership opportunities should exist in the staff and with all students in all year levels.

Keeping in touch with students

Students expressed a desire for principals to be accessible, approachable and familiar. They wanted to be able to talk with principals, to know them and be known by them. Students also recommended that principals make an effort to understand what goes on in the classroom and to mix with the 'general population' of the school. The large number of responses on this theme suggests a preference by students for personal contact with a friendly principal who understands their world because of his or her regular contact with it. Putting it lightly, in the words of one student:

> Principals should take note of the 'pal' in principal and really get to know the students as individuals, not just some, but the quiet average achievers as well as all the rebels.

Some of the students' comments carried interesting distinctions between leadership of the 'God Head' type and more distributive forms of leadership:

> Principals need to be amongst the students, not being merely figure heads. They ought to have close contact with their students and staff in order to have a school in harmony with itself.

Caring for and respecting students

Students not only appear to want regular contact with their principals, but also have expectations about the nature of this contact. The list of adjectives found in students' comments illustrates the kind of personal qualities recommended for principals – 'accessible', 'friendly', 'listening', 'helpful' and 'caring' appear frequently. Other words indicate what students do not like – 'the military dictator', an 'authoritarian position', a 'persecutor'. Students also expected principals to be responsible for their safety and protection. Some of the survey data illustrate the desire for a well managed, happy and safe school as a prime concern for students so that they have a good learning environment. Table 5.1 shows the students' top five priorities in relation to the management of the school. Percentage of responses are shown for each.

The impression created by Table 5.1 is of high expectations related to ensuring a safe, happy and secure environment. However, just over half of the students expected principals to encourage competition amongst students and amongst other schools.

Table 5.1 Students' top five priorities related to the management of the school

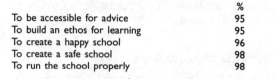

	%
To be accessible for advice	95
To build an ethos for learning	95
To create a happy school	96
To create a safe school	98
To run the school properly	98

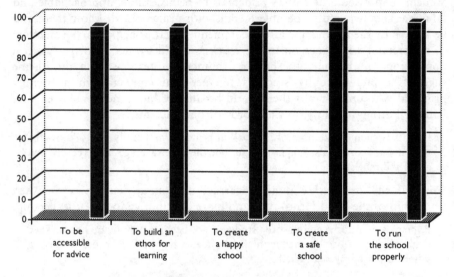

Disciplining disruptive students

Comments related to discipline and behaviour management were divided in their emphases. Some students were concerned that expulsion was used too readily while others had concerns that a tougher approach needed to be taken with disruptive students. A frequency count of comments in this category shows support for principals who take direct action to maintain order. Two responses illustrate the thoughts of students about school behaviour:

> In schools there is a huge disciplinary problem, even though this is not widely recognised. Juvenile crime rates are huge, and even though it is the parents' responsibility to look after their kids, the school should help out with this by using harsher punishments and more counselling with students who are continually badly misbehaving, abusing, destroying property etc.

> Our school is well led, but greater pressure on troublesome students would lead to a safer and more trouble-free environment.

Treating students equally

Student comments revealed concerns about inequality in the way they are perceived and treated at school. These concerns revolved around the selection of students for leadership positions. Two comments give the flavour of student concerns:

Students should be allowed to lead even though their culture and religion may be different from the norm.

I think many students feel cheated because they know that only a select few are given the opportunities to lead in the school.

The survey instrument contained several sections which enabled us to compare students' views with those of parents and teachers. Some of these data are now presented to identify common and competing expectations across the three groups.

Many of the expectations of principals held by students, parents and teachers are common to all groups, but there are also important differences. Table 5.2 presents a comparison of survey data on student, parent and teacher priorities for sixteen expectations related to concerns for students. The data in Table 5.2 show that students as a group ranked supportive aspects of the principal's role (items 1, 2 and 16) more highly than other more supervisory roles. However, they also assigned a significantly high priority (fourth) to the expectation that principals deal with serious discipline and behaviour problems.

Parents similarly gave highest priority to the item 'treat students as individuals' and also ranked the item 'provide role models for students' in their top three. They also included 'settling disputes and helping police investigate student misbehaviour' among their top five priorities. 'Developing students who can contribute to society' was given very high priority by parents. Teachers also gave top place to treating students as individuals. Like students and parents, teachers gave high priority to 'providing role models for students' and agreed with students that dealing with serious discipline and behaviour problems was a major priority. Along with parents, teachers included in their top five priorities the role of the principal as helping to

Table 5.2 A comparison of student, parent and teacher priorities on expectations of principals related to concern for students

I expect the principal:	Students	Parents	Teachers
to treat students as individuals	1	1	1
to give students opportunities to lead in the school	2	12	15
to provide a role model for students	3	3	5
to deal with serious discipline problems	4	9	3
to provide a safe refuge for students at risk	5	8	11
to ensure individual student needs are catered for	6	6	6
to develop students who can contribute to society	7	2	2
to know the students by name	8	10	8
to expel problem students	9	13	16
to consult with students on school rules	10	16	12
to understand students' home backgrounds	11	15	10
to settle student disputes	12	4	9
to report bad behaviour to parents	13	14	14
to involve students in community projects	14	10	13
to develop students who can be critical of society	15	7	4
to help police investigate student misbehaviour	16	4	7

develop students who can contribute to society (second highest for both teachers and parents) and also listed the item 'to develop students who can be critical of society' as a significant priority.

A number of common expectations are endorsed across all three groups. They include the supportive roles of the principal, treating students as individuals, and providing role models. At the same time, all three groups wanted principals to address serious behaviour issues in the school. Yet all three groups gave a lower priority to item 11 ('to expel problem students'), with teachers listing it last, parents thirteenth and students ninth.

Some interesting contrasts occur in relation to two items. With respect to item 13, teachers rated relatively highly 'to develop students who can be critical of society'. It was a role given less priority by parents and was significantly less important in the eyes of students. With respect to item 16, 'providing leadership opportunities for students', students made it their second highest priority while parents and teachers ranked it toward the lower end.

Summary

In summing up our analysis of student views, it is fair to say that there were many very favourable comments from students about school principals. Overall, students appear to expect leadership responsibilities to be shared across the school and have a strong interest in student leadership. Of their principals they expect regular, friendly contact and an understanding of the 'real world' of student and classroom life. They expect him or her to be caring about their students and to be responsible for their safety and protection. Also of concern to students is the issue of discipline with some split between those who expected more listening and less punishing and those who wanted swift action and stronger punishment. The latter view tended to figure more prominently. Students are concerned about issues of equity – particularly the perception of unfair treatment and bias in the selection of students for leadership positions.

EXPECTATIONS OF TEACHERS AND PARENTS

The expectations of teachers and parents figure prominently in the principals' thinking about school leadership and management. Here we summarise the expectations of teachers and parents about parent, teacher and community relations, the personal qualities of principals, school management, vision, values and futures orientation.

Parent, teacher and community relations

Our interviews included discussions of pressures, particularly pressures to develop trust and loyalty amongst staff while managing the roles of both independent arbitrator and consensus bringer. Principals were expected by parents, and by staff to a lesser extent, to manage and resolve internal

Table 5.3 Parent and teacher expectations on five items on staff relations

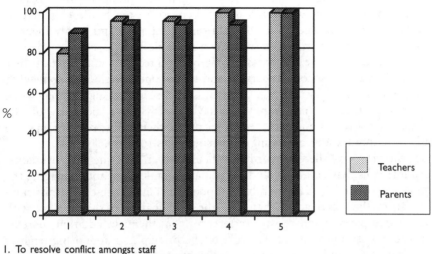

1. To resolve conflict amongst staff
2. To interact personally with staff about important issues
3. To demonstrate loyalty to school staff
4. To maintain high levels of trust with staff
5. To encourage staff to use their initiative

conflicts such as those that often occur between two groups of staff, young and old, traditional and progressive, staff who want change and staff who prefer the present or old way of operating. Some of the survey data reinforces these views, as Table 5.3 shows.

This table shows a high level of agreement among teachers that principals should demonstrate loyalty to staff and maintain high levels of trust with them, encourage them to use their initiative, interact personally on important issues, and be involved directly in conflict resolution. Parents and teachers also expected principals to be responsible for setting priorities for change, for improvements and upgrading.

The resolution of conflict is part of a communication theme linked with the expectation that principals express their vision clearly and communicate effectively with everyone in the school. Provision of clear direction is a very common expectation of both parents and teachers. It is frequently expressed as clear leadership vision and clear instructions. The high figures recorded on the relevant items in the survey results emphasise these views, outlined in Table 5.4.

Table 5.4 Parent and teacher expectations on four items on communication

I expect the principal to:	Parents (Strongly agree)	Teachers (Strongly agree)
listen to opinions	99%	100%
communicate effectively	100%	100%
express his or her vision clearly	97%	99%
advocate the school's values publicly	95%	96%

As mentioned earlier, the provision of clear direction by the principal is complicated by a feeling that teachers and parents should be able to take initiative in the school without constant recourse to the head. This matter, amongst others, is picked up in the data on consultation and involvement in school leadership and management shown in Table 5.5.

The generally positive responses by parents and teachers in respect of their own involvement in school leadership and management is clouded somewhat by the results on the last item in Table 5.5. This seems to suggest that while parents and teachers are happy to have parents and members of the community consulted and included by virtue of their skills, both groups are not of one mind about extending leadership roles to them.

For the principal, there are further difficulties that he or she must overcome if genuine consultation about, and participation in, leading and managing the school is to occur. The data in Table 5.6 point to some of these. One difficulty arises from the expectation that it is the principal who should deal with troublesome parents and resist interference from them. In addition, parents and teachers strongly support the role of the principal in appraising (eighty-seven per cent) and challenging staff (eighty-eight per cent). When these matters are taken into account, and when it is known that over eighty per cent of staff expect the principal to abide by staff decisions, the school leader must be careful about how participation in the school's affairs is handled.

In short, there is inherent conflict between the principal's management and leadership roles, institutional requirements and the expectations of parents

Table 5.5 Parent and teacher expectations on items on staff and parent participation in leadership and management.

I expect the principal to:	Parents (Strongly agree)	Teachers (Strongly agree)
consult with parents on management	70%	70%
include cultural groups in school management	66%	78%
give staff opportunities to lead in the school	97%	99%
provide staff opportunities to participate in management decisions	97%	98%
use the skills of parents in the school	99%	94%
give members of the community opportunities to lead in the school	56%	66%

Table 5.6 Expectations of parents and teachers on staff and parent relations

I expect the principal to:	Parents (Strongly agree)	Teachers (Strongly agree)
deal with difficult parents	93%	97%
resist parental interference	47%	58%
abide by staff decisions	67%	82%
take personal involvement in staff appraisal	99%	85%
challenge staff	87%	88%

and teachers. The data point to the extensive array of situations in which they have to address the competing expectations of these two groups.

Personal qualities

Most parents and teachers want the principal to respect the power of his or her position (ninety-eight per cent), to act fairly at all times (one hundred per cent) and to show personal values in leadership (ninety-two per cent). Almost ninety per cent of parents and teachers did not expect the principal to make major decisions alone and four fifths expect him or her to follow their personal views when making major decisions. These data suggest a troubling pathway for principals in making decisions in their schools. Parents and teachers, it would seem, prefer the principal to involve others in making major decisions and, at the same time, to demonstrate personal values and conscience in leadership. The dilemmas that these competing expectations can create for principals may go some way to explaining stress in leadership.

Management of the school

The delegation of authority, the acquisition of resources and the allocation of and accounting for funds, all figure prominently in parents' and teachers' expectations of their principals. The widest variation in priority was over the expectation that principals manage budgets. Parents placed this in their top five priorities while teachers had it in their bottom five. This may be explained partly by the fact that many teachers were participating in budget management in their departments or sections and partly because teachers may have felt that budget management should be carried out by school registrars, business managers or bursars. Parents, on the other hand, seem to hold the view that the principal, as the officer accountable for school expenditure, should have direct involvement in fiscal management.

Vision, values and futures orientation

Support for a futures orientation by principals was very strong amongst parents and teachers. They expected the principal to have a clear vision for the school (ninety-nine per cent), to be public about the school's values (ninety-six per cent), to plan strategically to achieve the vision (ninety-eight per cent), to give the lead in new directions for the school (ninety-five per cent) and to take into account the school's history when change was being contemplated (ninety-one per cent). Given these responses, it is not surprising that parents and teachers expect principals to attend national and international conferences (eighty-seven per cent) to renew and update their knowledge and to be active in national professional associations. These externally-focused activities are seen as enabling principals to continue their own learning and to build the professional networks necessary to gather information about possibilities for their schools. It is clear from these results that there is strong support for principals with a futures orientation.

3. EXPECTATIONS OF EXTERNAL STAKEHOLDERS

Our interviews corroborate the view that added pressures from external stakeholders are being felt by principals. The external stakeholders they referred to most often were the State Minister for Education and government education agencies and officers. Principals felt that schools were required to support government policies through implementation that, in the words of one, 'at least appears successful'.

Regional or diocesan offices were referred to frequently by government and Catholic school principals as stakeholders who expected trouble-free school leadership. Given that these offices usually play a significant role in the selection of principals and in shaping criteria for appointment and promotion, it is understandable that their expectations are keenly felt. In addition, principals also experienced pressures from their local communities.

They reported that they were expected by the community to uphold 'Australian values', to respond to local events and needs with quick action and to involve students in community projects. This expectation was further sharpened for Catholic and independent denominational schools. Bishops and parish priests are indirectly or directly responsible for selecting those who work in their schools and so they have particular expectations of principals' faith. Church-controlled councils are ever present stakeholders with expectations that the school not only be run as a faith community but that it set an example for the wider church community.

Government school principals spoke often about two major pressures – legislative and financial accounting compliance. Principals said that these pressures were the result of 'ever increasing bureaucratic demands'; having 'to do administration on behalf of the system'; changes emanating from political, social, educational, technical, industrial and economic sources in the environment; and the demands of politicians, cabinet directives and new systems like school-based management. This, although supposedly giving principals more power, allows the department to lay the blame for any failure at the principals' feet.

The external pressures experienced by principals are felt differently in different schools. Pressures include increasing competition with other schools, being available to police and family services when students are involved in crime or conflict and actively chasing enrolments and dealing with the press. Most principals reported that they felt financial pressures and the need to re-educate themselves in the business of generating funds, budgeting, resource allocation and 'generally battling to resource all of the needs of the school'.

All principals in our study confirmed that the nature of the school community impacts in some way on the leadership of the school. Language, culture and the socio-economic status of school community members were seen as influences which change the nature of school leadership. For example, in schools where a large proportion of students come from non-English speaking homes, principals have had to adjust by providing in-service training for teachers so as to help them teach these students. In schools where the cultural background of large numbers of students was not the same as the majority of the teachers, principals have adopted policies aimed at understanding cultural diversity and credibility with all cultural groups, actively acknowledging and listening to a range of needs. The socio-cultural background of the school community has direct influence on student and parent attitudes and in turn on the principal's leadership strategies.

The preceding discussion has emphasised that principals feel under constant pressure from a range of external stakeholders, some from the community closest to the school and some from agents and agencies linked with their employing authorities and government. It is not surprising then that our research uncovered a conservative attitude to change from parents and teachers.

THE MANAGEMENT OF CHANGE

The study findings present a complex picture of the management of change with both contradictions and commonalties embedded in data from students, parents and teachers. Table 5.7 shows the level of support which teachers, parents and students attach to the expectation that the principal should change the school.

Table 5.7 Expectations of teachers, students and parents on changing the school

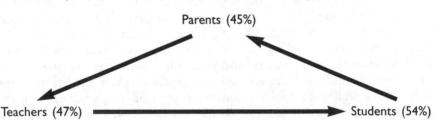

Table 5.8 Expectations of parents and teachers in relation to the management of change

I expect the principal to:	Parents (Strongly agree)	Teachers (Strongly agree)
respond to community pressures	45%	49%
meet the demands of politicians	12%	12%
change the dominant values in the school community	18%	15%
control the agenda of the school council	21%	32%
protect the school from external demands	99%	98%
keep change to a minimum	67%	82%
prioritise issues of change	97%	96%
introduce change slowly	78%	78%

The leadership issue here is how to balance division over the pursuit of change agendas, whatever their source. Other data from the study shown in Table 5.8 point to a very cautious approach by parents and teachers in relation to the principal's role as change agent, particularly change initiated outside the school.

Table 5.8 shows that most parents and teachers expect the principal not to respond consistently to the demands of politicians. However, most changes in schools, whether on the curriculum or structural fronts, come from political initiatives which result in legislative or regulatory change. Perhaps parents and teachers are wary of the transitory nature of political imperatives and want principals to choose what is good for their school and its children as a first priority. Perhaps parents and teachers are uttering a cry for a moratorium on changes emanating from party political platforms; or they may be expressing disenchantment with the level of political intervention in school curriculum and management.

Few parents and teachers want the principal to control the school council agenda. This is an interesting post-script to the findings on partnerships in school management and decision-making among parents, teachers and principals. It reinforces the view that where parents are involved in formal school structures, both they and the teachers believe they should be allowed to operate free from manipulation or control by the school principal.

Parents and teachers expect the principal to protect the school from unrealistic external demands and where this is not possible, they expect sound management of the demands within the school.

They see the principal as the agent responsible for prioritising change while parents and teachers seem to expect the principal to adopt the role of 'gate keeper'. Outside influences impacting on the school include curriculum directions set by the system, assessment and accountability requirements, or legislation obliging schools to workplace activity of specific kinds.

In the role of 'gate keeper', the principal seems to be expected to know what the external issues are, to determine what is unnecessary and to sort and prioritise initiatives appropriate to the school. This implies that the principal be skilled in analysis and synthesis with the wisdom to make decisions about what should and should not be allowed to impact on the school. Such expectations seem to contradict the sharing of power among parents, teachers and community members as discussed earlier in this section. However, demands for participation suggest involvement but without obligation and consequence.

To sum up, the interplay of expectations about change with how parents and teachers think principals should act, creates tensions which add to the complexity of the leadership role. These are compounded where governments and system authorities operate on an understanding that the principal is their 'branch manager' and parents and school council members believe that he or she is their Chief Executive Officer.

Overall, the distinctive feature in Table 5.9 is that those close to the school have fairly predictable expectations of their principals. Parents and teachers attach greatest importance to good management of the school, followed closely by sound staff, parent and community relations, the principal's personal qualities and a commitment to concern for students. Expectations related to vision, values and futures orientation were considered of lesser importance.

The management of change was a distant last, an outcome which stands in stark contrast to the kinds of expectations which authorities outside the school have of principals. Those expectations are firmly fixed on the principal as change agent, restructuring advocate, efficient manager and mediator between external demands and local wishes. Expectations of students, parents and teachers are focused on enhancing the learning experience and environment, sound and supportive staff relationships and the creation of a well-managed, happy school. Such a contrast pinpoints the conundrum mentioned earlier. It also exposes tensions when it comes to enhancing the principal's professional practice. The strength of this conundrum should not be underestimated. When leading locally is framed and constrained by system policies and priorities, school principals can become the 'meat' in an unpalatable sandwich (Dymock, 1996).

Table 5.9 Parents' and teachers' rank order for six categories of expectations

	%
Management of the school	27
Staff, parent and community relations	22.8
Personal qualities	21.1
Concern for students	20
Visions, values and orientation	6.7
Management of change	2.5

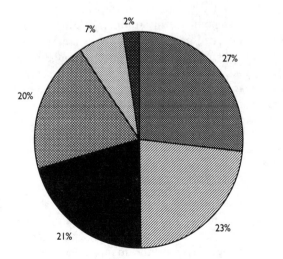

- Management of the school
- Staff, parent and community relations
- Personal qualities
- Concern for students
- Visions, values and orientation
- Management of change

4. LEARNING FROM THE STUDY

Since one of the key purposes of this study was to inform the professional development of principals, there are three implications that can be drawn from the results.

First, findings from our study indicate that principals need to concentrate their learning on immediate functional issues affecting the smooth running of schools: developing knowledge and skills about ways to create the right kind of climate in which learning can take place; learning more about students themselves, their needs and aspirations; pursuing personal improvement in communication within the school community; and acquiring the micro-political skills to ensure that the interests of stakeholders are accommodated in what the school does. These are all important elements in the professional development of school leaders.

Second, developing the necessary self-confidence to withstand the stresses and strains encountered when external and internal priorities conflict is essential for the well-being of a modern principal. Refining, understanding and confirming the educational values that lie at the heart of consistent decision-making are important components of principals' professional learning. A set of professional values is necessary if principals are to mediate productive settlements in contradictory situations (this subject is taken further in Chapter 8 which deals with the ethical challenges principals face). In addition, knowing and being able to apply processes which spread involvement in decision-making and knowing when to invite initiative and when to take decisions alone are critical capacities for principals.

Third, principals must address their attitudes to change and a futures orientation. Principals have no way of making their schools immune from the influences of governments, educational policy-makers and members of the wider worlds of business, industry and commerce. As a consequence, school leaders must not allow their professional development to be seduced by the functional issues referred to in the first point in this summary. Life is easier when the status quo is undisturbed but leading schools is about creating the circumstances to achieve preferred goals and to do so requires a concern for doing at least some things differently. Principals' learning must embrace the vision and values inherent in innovation and the requirements of mandated change. More than this, principals should be committed to the expansion of theoretical and practical knowledge about how to bring new ideas to fruition in their schools.

CONCLUSION

From the findings in our study, there is little doubt that school leadership is subject to a range of competing expectations. Principals recognise and worry about how to manage the macro and micro-political realities within which they work. The control of school change agendas, the management of role conflicts intrinsic to mediating external demands whilst maintaining high staff and parent trust and the need to show concern for student experience are central to strong school leadership. All combine to make the principal's life challenging.

Politics is about resolving competing expectations among groups with particular interests; it is about knowing where the weight of opinion lies. In short, it is about gaining the numbers to ensure that a critical mass of support is present when hard decisions have to be made or when new directions are entertained and taken. How principals reconcile their personal values, visions and goals with some of the contradictions they face from different internal and external interest groups is a continuous struggle for them. Chapter 8 takes up this theme and offers some practical suggestions to facilitate action.

REFERENCES

Angus, L. (1992) Local school management and the politics of participation, *Unicorn*, Vol. 18, no. 2, pp. 4–16.

Dymock, C. (1996) Dilemmas for school leaders and administrators in restructuring, in K. Leithwood, J. Chapman, D. Corson, P. Hallinger and A. Hart (eds.) *International Handbook of Educational Leadership and Administration*, Vol. 1, Kluwer, Dordrecht.

Hilmer, G. F. (1995) *National Competition Policy: Report of the Independent Committee of Inquiry*, Australian Government Printer, Canberra.

Logan, L., Sachs, J. and Dempster, N. (1996) *Planning for Better Primary Schools*, The Australian College of Education, Canberra.

Marginson, S. (1996) Effects of the abolition of the new schools policy. Paper given at the Council Seminar, The Australian College of Education, Canberra, March.

Marginson, S. (1977) *Educating Australia: government, economy and citizen since 1960*, Cambridge University Press, Cambridge.

Peach, F. (1996) Leading schools. Paper given at the Professional Development and Training Framework for Principals Conference, Department of Education, Surfers' Paradise, Queensland, March.

Queensland Government (1996) *Report of the Commission of Audit*, Government Printer, Brisbane.

Smyth, J. (1996) The socially just alternative to the 'self-managing School', in K. Leithwood et al., (eds.) *International Handbook of Educational Leadership and Administration*, Vol 2, Kluwer, Dordrecht.

Townsend, T. (1996) School effectiveness and improvement initiatives and the restructuring of education in Australia, School *Effectiveness and Improvement*, Vol. 17, no. 2, pp. 114–132.

Yeatman, A. (1993) Corporate managerialism and the shift from the welfare to the competition state, *Discourse*, Vol. 13, no. 2, pp. 3–9.

6

Some Comparative Learnings from the Study

Leif Moos and Neil Dempster

INTRODUCTION

Chapters 3, 4 and 5 have presented and discussed data from our studies in England, Scotland, Denmark and Australia. Although the Australian study employed slightly different approaches to data gathering from those in the other three countries, the purposes and key questions in all four studies were similar. As a consequence, in this chapter we analyse the overall findings for similarities and differences and we discuss some of the significant impressions we gained from our work. In our analysis, three frames of reference are influential: leadership and the cultural context; 'new public management' and change. Although they have been mentioned in earlier chapters, we revisit each in turn briefly, to remind readers of some of the concepts around which our study has turned. Secondly, we synthesise major messages about school leadership, identifying those aspects that are tightly context bound and those that cross cultural boundaries. We conclude by acknowledging that cultural differences are to be valued in the perennial quest to learn more about leadership in our own settings.

LEADERSHIP AND THE CULTURAL CONTEXT

In our work we were constantly reminded that leadership is, in large part, a cultural phenomenon. Being a leader in Australian politics or religion is different from being a political or religious leader in England or Denmark. So, being a school leader differs according to the norms and values of the society and the local community which the school serves. The growth of Scottish schools from a religious base has left a mark on the leadership role there, while the democratic and communitarian spirit evident in Denmark influences how an individual leads the Danish school. The English 'class culture' has shaped and continues to shape leadership in that country. Of course, there are infinite variations in leadership because the local cultural context within all four countries also contributes to what is possible and acceptable at any given time.

Leadership like any other social practice, therefore, is context bound. The ways leaders perceive their circumstances, their jobs and the way they see themselves play a decisive part in moulding how they perform. One major source of influence on their perceptions is their own expectations and the expectations of their educational partners (politicians, local community members, parents, school boards, teachers and students). These expectations – together with structural features and macro- and micro-political demands – contribute to the culture within which leaders interpret their role and functions. Leaders do not perform solely as a response to official dicta or standards required of them by governmental or local authority regulations. These requirements and standards may not be the final arbiter in contexts where the school is insulated from official 'interference' by a culture of community cohesion or historical diffidence. Given the premise that leadership is a characteristic of the cultural milieu, we turn to discuss some of what we have learned from our research.

SOME LEARNINGS FROM THE STUDY ABOUT LEADERSHIP AND THE CULTURAL CONTEXT

Consistent with our description above, we have learned much about the influence of both macro- and micro-cultures on schools and school leadership. For example, at the macro level, the very way in which an education system is shaped and legitimised by the Act of Parliament was drawn to our attention during the project.

We examined the Acts of Parliament in the four countries of our study, providing us with an interesting insight into some of the assumptions which underpin the provision of public schooling. It also puts into sharper comparative perspective the relationship between parents and schools in the education of children. From the timing of the Acts, we may begin to infer differences in the way heads might approach the leadership of their schools. For example, in England and Wales, the Act of 1988 states:

> It shall be the duty of the parents of every child of compulsory school age to cause him (sic) to receive full-time education suitable to his age, ability and aptitude, either by regular attendance at school or otherwise
> (Education Act (England and Wales) section 76, 1988).

This places responsibility on parents to send their children to school and sees this as synonymous with 'full-time education'. It fails to recognise the direct role of parents in the process, although the 'otherwise' clause, as it is known, has provided a loophole for parents to educate their children as an alternative to school attendance.

The Scottish Act, although bearing strong similarities to the English/Welsh Act, makes parents responsible for ensuring an 'efficient education' and is similar to the English/Welsh Act in its inclusion of a 'by other means' clause:

> It shall be the duty of the parent of every child of school age to provide efficient education for him suitable to his age, ability and aptitude either by causing him to attend the public school regularly or by other means
>
> (The Education (Scotland) Act, 1980 Chapter 44, Part 11, Section 30).

Neither of these Acts, although formed during a period of growing 'parent power', includes any notion of partnership, in sharp contrast to the Danish Act of 1993 which places parents at the centre of the educational process and implies for school leaders a need to build this partnership into their teaching and management of the school community:

> The task of the basic school is, in co-operation with parents, to offer possibilities for the pupils to acquire knowledge, skills, working methods and forms of expression which contribute to the all-round development of the individual pupil.
>
> (Folkeskole Act of 1993, article 1.1)

The differences signalled by these Acts appear to account for differences in how managerialism and models of leadership in education have been interpreted. A less centralised, tightly framed, regulatory framework would seem to fit within the Danish tradition of democratic participation which, throughout the project, was explicitly mentioned by Danish heads as something to be valued and retained.

A comparison with the Education Act from Queensland, Australia, shows marked similarities with the UK Acts. The Queensland Act states:

> Every parent of a child being of the age of compulsory attendance shall cause that child to be enrolled at a State school; or to be enrolled at a non-State school; and to attend the State school or non-State school, on every school day, for the program of instruction for which the child is enrolled, unless there is in existence at the material time, in respect of that child, a dispensation or provisional dispensation granted in accordance with section 115.
>
> (Queensland Education [General Provisions] Act 1989).

The similarities with the tone of the English Act is hardly surprising given the fact that Queensland was, for more than a century, a colony of Great Britain. The Act does not spell out a role for either the child or the parent, the implication being that the school is responsible for the nature of the instruction the child receives as well as for the way in which that instruction will be managed throughout the school year.

What is clear from our analysis of the study data in the light of the four Education Acts is that leadership practice seems to carry much of the intent of the legislators in each country. What stands out, however, is that Denmark's school leaders recognise instinctively a rightful place for parents in the education process and the school's responsibility as a key contributor to the maintenance and development of democracy.

The idea that models of leadership are influenced by the culture and traditions of a country is further illustrated in the way schools are structured.

Our analysis of the study data suggests that UK schools are strongly hierarchical, reflecting the wider society. In larger secondary schools, it is not uncommon to find seven or eight levels of status and hierarchy: head, deputy heads, assistant heads, senior teachers, heads of department, deputy heads of department, mainscale teachers with particular responsibilities and teachers with little responsibility beyond their classroom management.

By contrast in Denmark, there has been a long tradition of flat structures consisting of the leadership team (head and deputy) and teachers. Leaders have often emerged from the once-powerful Teachers' Council, bringing with them values which accord high levels of trust to their colleagues' professionalism. This 'flatarchy' is gradually being transformed in many schools (including the schools in our project) because of what are seen as difficulties in 'leading' so many staff. However, rather than moving towards a UK-type hierarchy, Danish heads, parents and teachers seem to be favouring project-group structures (akin to the features of a starburst organisation) because this is more consonant with a collaborative, democratic tradition and culture. The 'starburst' organisation requires teachers to work in teams, at times across the curriculum, and to teach and assess through project work.

In Australia, the organisational structure is closer to the Scottish model. Nonetheless, our data showed that in Queensland, there are strong expectations that leadership should be shared with teachers and students. In fact, the distribution of leadership responsibility beyond those in positional authority to those in the 'ranks' is a common cultural phenomenon in 'egalitarian' Australia. The demand for participative leadership did not seem to be quite so evident in English or Scottish schools.

NEW PUBLIC MANAGEMENT

Osborne and Gaebler (1992) have argued that there is a new paradigm in the management of the public sector. However, there is growing evidence that different countries, and different segments of the public sector in those countries, have introduced their own forms of NPM according to their diverse historical and cultural traditions, political agendas and economic conditions (Dunleavy and Hood, 1994; Pollitt and Summa, 1996; Ferlie et al., 1996).

The effects of these varieties of New Public Management (NPM) have been felt to differing degrees in all four countries. According to Ferlie, there are four types of NPM evident in the management and administration of the public sector worldwide. These they call NPM Models 1, 2, 3 and 4 (see endnote) which they have given the following names: (1) The Efficiency Drive; (2) Downsizing and Decentralisation; (3) In Search of Excellence; and (4) Public Service Orientation. Using this typology, we suggest that England in its approach to education policy clearly follows Model 1 while Australia and Scotland seem to exhibit features of Model 2 in their educational reforms. Denmark seems to be oriented towards many of the elements of Model 4.

Despite these differences, all four countries have experienced trends such as

- moves towards school self-management;
- the imposition of greater demands for financial accountability;
- the increase of consumer control over what goes on in schools;
- the expectation that schools expose their performance to public scrutiny; and
- increasing pressure for outcomes-based assessment of students, principals and teachers.

These trends have come into the schools in the four countries in 'wolf's or sheep's clothing', often mandated by governments or educational policy-makers and administrators. When in wolf's clothing, reform was sudden and severe as in England and Wales with the 1988 Education Reform Act; when in sheep's clothing it was slow and measured as in Queensland, Australia and in Denmark where the demand for change has taken longer to gain momentum. We discuss these claims and indicate some of our reasons for making them below.

SOME LEARNINGS FROM THE STUDY ABOUT LEADERSHIP AND NEW PUBLIC MANAGEMENT

There is growing evidence that the market driven policies of the UK have produced not only greater degrees of inequity for school students, but also that the form in which policy making processes take place has become increasingly centralised (Mahony and Hextall, 1997). The discourse of globalisation has been significant in legitimating this in the UK and the compliance-oriented bureaucratic traditions in England and Wales seem to have presented little resistance. This is also the case in Australia where the decentralisation of leadership and management authority and responsibility has been accompanied by the tightening of systemic controls consistent with the NPM trends mentioned above. Although somewhat protected by the Scottish Office, heads who participated in our study were just as critical as their English and Australian colleagues of the impact of policies accompanying devolution competition, central facets of NPM.

Our work with Danish heads provided a very interesting counter example of how demands for change in the management of the public sector can be conceptualised very differently at school and community levels. The negativity with which English, Scottish and Australian heads reported on the impact of NPM on their schools was not so evident amongst their Danish counterparts. They seemed to have ways of coping with NPM which provided an alternative to the centralisation/decentralisation duality experienced in the other three countries. Part of the explanation for this lies in the fact that Denmark has not followed the ideology of NPM with the degree of 'purity' evident in the

United Kingdom, or for that matter, Australia (there, some differences exist in the various States in the degree to which the impact of NPM has been felt in schools). Another explanation can be put down to the strong 'community ownership' of Danish schools. We formed the view that this sense of ownership helped to quarantine schools from some of the NPM changes which had been injected into other aspects of the Danish public sector. A third explanation lies in the strength of commitment Danish schools have to democratic participation by their most immediate stakeholders. Having a voice in what policies should be accepted inside the school gate remains a firm part of the Danish school agenda.

The contrast between Denmark and the other three countries in our study, with regard to the intrusion of NPM into school leadership and management practices highlighted the school's role in educating future citizens. It raises sharply the issue of their rights to participate in an inclusive model of political decision-making. The Danes seem to have held to this responsibility much more effectively than have English, Scottish and Australian heads. In these three countries, NPM policies and practices have restricted the role of schools and removed their educational mission while lamenting this retrogressive influence. School leaders at system and local levels have, nonetheless, accepted the tenets of NPM, apparently without demur. Yet to do so ignores the responsibility of schools to develop their students' capacity for democratic deliberation, critical judgement and rational understanding, with the danger that future generations of democratic citizens will disappear'. Schools in Denmark have help at hand when faced with policy compliance, help which does not seem to be available in the United Kingdom or Australia. Article 3 of the Danish Folkeskole Act (1993) states:

> The school shall prepare the students for participation, sharing of responsibilities, rights and duties in a society with freedom and democracy. The education in the school as well as the daily life of the school therefore must build on intellectual liberty, equality and democracy.

Because of this requirement, it is widely accepted in Denmark that students should be participants in decisions about their education and that teachers and heads should provide role models for them by acting in a democratic way. Collaboration between students and teachers and between teachers and heads is expected. In a speech in August 1997, the Danish Minister for Education, Ole Vig Jensen, was most direct in rejecting a model of education based on the kind of economic rationalism which has underpinned so much of education policy in the UK and Australia:

> A democratic challenge to education is the way to go if we want to develop our democracy. If an education must prepare for democracy, it must be democratically organised. Our educational system shall not be a product of a global educational race without thinking of the goals and ideals we want in Denmark. We don't postulate a connection between democracy and education. We insist on it.

This statement provides a reaffirmation of the nexus between education and democracy in Denmark and underpins current educational reform. It is now likely that heads will become even more concerned with teaching and learning, not through the kinds of outcome-monitoring practices introduced in the UK and Australia but through supervising teacher teams in planning, teaching and evaluating their classroom practice. The responsibility of the 'leader' will be to assist teachers in becoming more 'professional', most critically with regard to their classroom practice and ethics. The other role for the head will be to provide 'organisational leadership', focusing on the whole school development as a learning organisation. In this, leaders will be responsible for initiating and maintaining dialogue with staff, students, the school board, parents and the community about values and goals. They will also be charged with working through the inevitable conflicts which arise over different interpretations of these. Though there are some dangers in unquestioned preconceptions about what constitutes 'community' (Clarke and Newman, 1997), the Danish interpretation would seem to offer hope to those increasingly concerned about some of the negative effects of NPM.

This analysis leads us to argue that the Danish approach stands out as distinct at a time when the 'globalisation' of educational policy, constructed to favour NPM in its varying forms, seems to have carried all before it. The views of Smyth (1996) endorse the Danish stand:

> I want to propose that if schools are to be saddled with what appear to be mandated forms of self-management, then this ought to occur on a very different theoretical and philosophical terrain than is happening at the moment – one that is less driven by economic agenda, and that is more informed by educational, social, and dare I say it, democratic ideals.
>
> (Smyth, 1996, p. 1101)

In the United Kingdom, the government's plans for NPM stress the head's role beyond the school itself – working in the community, promoting the image of the school and taking part in national initiatives. All of these are seen as necessary if the school is to be transformed to take a competitive position in the marketplace while working to the government's educational agenda. Notwithstanding this policy imperative, parents, teachers and boards in the United Kingdom rated the external role of the head as a very low priority for them. This is not surprising because, in general, our data showed that issues closest to the school were considered highest in priority in all countries. For example, in Australia, there was a clear hierarchy of expectations – local first, regional next with state and national. Danish teachers, like those in the United Kingdom and Australia, did not rank the out-of-school demands on heads highly. They agreed with parents and boards that the head should stay 'close at hand in school'. The 'in-school professionals', teachers and heads are, it appears, expected to see themselves as members of a school culture and therefore to be sometimes 'purposefully blind' to the demand for progress from outsiders.

In Denmark during the period of the study, there was not the same strong pressure as in the United Kingdom or Australia to move the school system into a market economy. Danish parents and boards fiercely rejected the idea. The smack of competition which they saw in promoting the image of one school over another was not an acceptable proposition.

To sum up, our study has led us to the view that NPM is not an absolute concept. It is not a mandated global imperative. It is forced to change when confronted with the demands of different cultural settings, and when people resist the pressures of the 'universal product' (Hampden-Turner and Trompenaars, 1993).

CHANGE

The concept of externally mandated change has been of particular interest in our research. However, because our studies were school-focused we were equally interested in school-initiated change and changes brought about by pressures from local community circumstances. By externally mandated change we mean the policies and practices injected into schooling systems in all four countries by governments – policies and practices carrying the sanctions of civil or public service authorities. By school-initiated change, we mean the new things schools do in response to immediately felt needs or heart felt aspirations. School-initiated change is discretionary, requiring local leadership, local agreement and local effort to make the change a reality. Likewise change in response to local community circumstances is often necessitated by movements in demography, shifts in public attitudes or social practices introduced into the school's immediate environment.

SOME LEARNINGS FROM THE STUDY ABOUT LEADERSHIP AND CHANGE

Modern leadership theory contains much about leaders as change managers because of the rapidly changing environment with which we are all faced. Although it is almost a truism that change is now a constant, resistance to change seems to be just as perennial a concept, though its application differs from country to country. Parents, boards and teachers rated change management by heads quite low in priority both in the United Kingdom and Denmark while in Australia parents, teachers and students, ranked changing the school as the least important in the list of the expectations of the head.

Given that most schools are essentially conservative in nature, it is not surprising that the demands on heads to become more corporate like, more market-place oriented and more outward-looking are rejected by parents and boards. This was the case in all four countries. The message was clear – the head should attend to his or her responsibilities within the school as a first priority. One of those priorities was the head's responsibility to help the teachers to keep up-to-date. Parents and boards in all countries found this to be a prominent part of the head's job.

Part of the reason for the lack of a strong commitment to change from within the school may be because the head is seen as a person who develops 'a vision for the school' and who has the necessary management skills to carry it out with and through others. Notwithstanding this 'futures oriented' expectation, our impression in all four countries is one of people wanting their heads to be locally focused, motivated by internal matters and driven by those 'hands-on' practical concerns which are felt most keenly by teachers, parents and children. These are not the substance of the kinds of far-reaching future oriented 'visionary' changes so often sought by authorities external to the school.

Nevertheless, school 'vision' is ranked highly in the United Kingdom as it is in each of the other countries. From the evidence in our study, we know that the English and Scottish teachers, parents and board members use the term to indicate the head's ability to advocate a clear direction for the school. We are left with the impression that the pursuit of a vision may be seen by many close to these schools as a means of ensuring continuity in practice rather than as a means of achieving anything radically different.

The Danish teachers ranked 'vision' highly too, but they seemed to have a distinctive understanding of the term. For them it implied that the head should build and maintain a dialogue with the staff and other groups about the direction, the values and the culture that the school should develop. However, there was no evidence in the study to suggest that Danish parents and teachers were more readily disposed to change than their European colleagues across the North Sea. The position in Australia was little different. In fact, our data on expectations related to change and setting new futures for the school reinforced the essential conservatism of school communities in that part of the southern hemisphere.

In summing up this part of the chapter, it is clear to us that the similarities in tradition and political heritage in England, Scotland and Australia have highlighted Danish differences in approaches to school leadership. Nevertheless, our analysis has pointed out what is distinctive in each of these countries and suggested why this is so. We now turn to the task of synthesising some of the major messages we have taken from our work.

A SYNTHESIS

The final part of the chapter affords us an opportunity to synthesise some of our learnings from the study into a series of propositions which may guide thinking about school leadership in different parts of the world. We have identified seven propositions which we believe are grounded in our findings.

Proposition 1. The cultural context counts

We are now further disposed to the view that generic approaches to the development of leadership capacity are flawed. Our study of what people expect of their school leaders, from inside and outside the school, has reinforced for us the fundamental influence of the cultural context. It has a clear and direct impact on how leadership is conceived and how people feel it should be carried out. Recipes for becoming 'the good school leader' ignore the need for understanding what is possible within the political, social and historical constraints of school systems in different countries. Even though global trends associated with New Public Management and the change agenda that goes with it seem to be cross-cultural phenomena, we have no doubt about the foolishness of transplanting, for example, an Australian principal into a Danish school with the expectation that he or she could lead just as well as in a home environment. In other words, there is no magic transnational formula for school leadership. Leadership knowledge comes with cultural experience. So we would argue that, ideally, the school leader should be a student of culture – in a sense, a lay anthropologist pursuing both macro- and micro-cultural understanding.

Proposition 2. Effective school leaders are not just managers

The idea that an effective leader requires more than good management skill is consistent with Proposition 1. Our research has shown us that the definition of effective leadership in schools differs from culture to culture even though all members of the school community might agree with the need for school leaders to be professional about what they do. In England, heads are expected to act as behavioural role models; in Scotland, they are expected to be directly involved in supporting teaching and learning in the classroom with extensive curriculum knowledge; in Denmark they must have pedagogical insight but provide support at a distance for their teachers; in Australia, they are expected to demonstrate the strength of their personal qualities as they extend leadership and management opportunities to their teachers.

Proposition 3. Leadership values are essential

The Australian study showed that heads are expected to demonstrate clear personal and professional values in the way they lead their schools. This was a consistent theme in each of the other three countries. The nature of those values, however, was again dependent upon the cultural context within which the leader worked. In short, there are no universal school leadership values which can be exported or imported at will. Although the study findings showed that there are some generally agreed professional values which are common to all – for example, a concern for student's learning, partnerships with parents and public accountability – the way in which these values are played out differs from one country to another. The importance of leadership values is brought into stark relief when the head is confronted with difficult decisions involving students, parents or policy makers. Strong leadership values provide a basis for the head to act consistently in circumstances which present contradictions.

Proposition 4. Local sites are significant in leading a school

There are cultures within cultures (Giddens, 1984) and this is nowhere more evident than in the organisations human beings create to carry out their daily activities. Schools develop cultures of their own within the broader cultural settings in which they are located. The culture of the school carries within it values and norms influencing how things are done and why they are done in particular ways. When a new leader is appointed to a school, he or she moves into a new sub-cultural milieu and what might have been possible in a previous appointment may now prove impossible. Understanding the expectations of the school's stakeholders is essential if heads are to learn how to lead and manage the school effectively. This does not mean compromising personal and professional values but it does mean that what works in one school won't necessarily work in another.

Proposition 5. Shared leadership is an increasing expectation

The Danish data emphasise the participative role that teachers and students play with their heads in leading the school. The expectation of a democratic partnership which also includes parents is embedded in the Danish school system. This was not so evident in England, Scotland and Queensland. There, the move to involve parents and community members in School Councils has added a veneer of shared leadership to schools but rather more in a managerial capacity than a democratic one. However, we are of the view that there is sufficient evidence from the study to contend that teachers, parents and students are increasingly seeking a greater say in decisions about the school. In short, they want bureaucratic approaches to leadership to be replaced by distributed leadership throughout the school. We acknowledge that implementing 'distributed leadership' must be worked through in appropriate ways in different countries, but we are firmly of the view that in a collegial setting such as a school, moving in this direction is essential.

Proposition 6. Leaders are often faced with contradiction

Our work with heads during the study revealed the extent of the competing demands they face – demands which are often contradictory in nature. Taking a course of action which benefits the school as a whole while it disadvantages a small number of students is one such contradiction. Devoting extensive time to one parent thus denying access to a larger number is another. Advertising for students to assist in improving enrolments while reducing the viability of a neighbouring school is a third. Issues like these and many others put the school leader in an unenviable position. How decision-making consistency is maintained when contradictory situations are encountered looms large in their minds. Our research suggest that heads are increasingly meeting these types of situations and they are often left alone to manage as best they can. Living with contradiction so that professional integrity and self-worth are maintained is a prominent feature of contemporary leadership.

Proposition 7. Internal and external priorities compete for leaders' resolution

Those priorities that arise in the school from those closest to it, we have referred to as school initiated; those that arise remote from the school in central offices or through government policy we call externally mandated. Our work has re-emphasised the fact that both types of priorities come into conflict at the school gate and that it is the head who is expected to reach a resolution. The problem is that the system expects the head to resolve in favour of its priorities while at the school the local priority is meant to win the day. Many leaders in the project felt they were crunched between NPM demands for efficiency and control on one hand and educational demands for effective and sensible education on the other hand. At the same time the students claimed new kinds of learning opportunities and opportunities for personal development that are not in accordance with national standards. There is constant tension surrounding this competition and heads need sophisticated political skills to negotiate solutions acceptable to their political masters and to their constituents. Making judgements about where one's loyalties lie when deciding between proximal and distal priorities will continue to test the values of the head.

CONCLUSION

Throughout the study, it was enlightening to work with researchers and heads whose views of leadership in their own countries were expanded by the data gathered in the four countries involved. Three of these are very close to each other, while the fourth, Australia, is separated by great distance. However, such is the pervasiveness of educational change that there was much in common for us to research. It is the results and our interpretation of them which have re-emphasised the cultural differences amongst us. We say that this is healthy. No global force or movement should hold such sway over public policy making that schools, schooling and school leadership become 'cloned' throughout the world. We think that there is benefit to students, teachers, parents and the countries in which they live in accepting cultural differences for what they can teach us about ourselves. So we say: "Watch – don't copy!"

ENDNOTE

Characteristics of the four models are listed below

NPM Model 1: The Efficiency Drive

Core themes include:

• an increased attention of financial control; getting more from less
• management by hierarchy; a 'command and control' mode of working
• an extension of audit, both financial and professional
• increased stress on provider responsiveness to consumers
• deregulation of the labour-market and increasing the pace of work
• a reduction in the self regulating power of the professions
• new forms of corporate governance; moves to a board of directors model.

NPM Model 2: Downsizing and Decentralisation

Core themes include:

• an extension to more elaborate and developed quasi-markets
• a move to management by contract
• a split between a small strategic core and a large operational periphery
• a split between public funding and independent sector provision; the emergence of separate purchaser and provider organisations
• moves to new management styles, such as management by influence; stress on strategic alliances between organisations.

NPM Model 3: In Search of Excellence

Core themes include:

• strong emphasis on the importance of organisational culture
• highlights the role of values, culture, rites, and symbols in shaping how people actually behave at work
• strong interest in how organisations manage change and innovation.

NPM Model 4: Public Service Orientation

Core themes include:

• a major concern with service quality
• reflection of user (rather than customer) concerns and values in the management process
• a desire to shift power back from appointed to elected local bodies
• scepticism as to the role of markets in public services

- stress on the development of societal learning over and above the delivery of routine services
- a continuing set of distinctive public service tasks and values.

REFERENCES

Clarke, J. and Newman, J. (1997) *The Managerial State*, Sage, London.

Dunleavy, P. and Hood, C. (1994) From old public administration to New Public Management, *Public Money and Management*. July–September, pp. 9–16.

Ferlie, E., Ashburner, L. and Pettigrew, A. (1996) *The New Public Management in Action*, Oxford University Press, Oxford.

Giddens, A. (1984) *The Constitution of Society*, Polity Press, Cambridge.

Hampden-Turner, C. and Trompenaars, F. (1993) *The Seven Cultures of Capitalism*, Doubleday, New York.

Mahony, P. and Hextall, I. (1997) *The Policy Context and Impact of the TTA: A Summary*, Roehampton Institute, London.

Osborne, A. and Gaebler, T. (1992) *Reinventing Government: How the Entrepreneurial Spirit is Transforming the Public Sector*, Addison Wesley, Reading, Mass.

Pollitt, C. and Summa, H. (1996) Trajectories of reform: public management change in four countries. Paper given to the Public Services Management 2000 Conference, University of Glamorgan, 11 October.

Smyth, J. (1996) The socially just alternative to the self-managing school, in K. Leithwood et al. (eds.) *International Handbook of Educational Leadership and Administration*, Kluwer, Dordrecht.

7

Who Really Runs the School?

Pat Mahony, John MacBeath and Leif Moos

INTRODUCTION

'The headteacher runs the school. If anything goes wrong it gets put down to her fault.' So wrote one of the pupils in our study, reflecting a fairly widely-held view of where the buck stops and where the power and decision-making lie. Certainly from a pupil's eye view it would appear that the headteacher was both prime and final mover. The deeper question 'who really runs the school?' deserves a more complex answer.

English schools have had their own Boards of Governors since 1980, but not until 1988 did they acquire the far-reaching powers and responsibilities which they now enjoy. In the words of Michael Golby 1988 marks the end of 'ceremonial governorship' and the beginning of hands-on running of schools. Boards of Governors were put in place to ensure a greater accountability, to represent other constituencies (parents and community) and to attenuate the previously far-reaching powers of the headteacher. They have a central role in policy-making, development planning and accountability, quite different from their Scottish and Danish counterparts who may advise the headteacher on policy, may or may not be involved in development planning and, by dint of their limited powers, are accountable primarily in a moral sense.

Scotland has always kept a close watching brief on what was happening in England as well as other countries, Denmark being one with which it has had a strong historic relationship. When School Boards were introduced in 1989 in Scotland, they took a carefully-considered, different path from the English/Welsh models, and one much closer to that of Denmark.

Whereas the function of 'governors' was to govern, school board 'members' were seen as providing a channel or bridge between parents and teachers, on the one hand carrying information from the school to the parent body and on the other providing a forum for parents' issues to be raised and representing the views of parents to school management. Apart from their one hand on the lever of power (involvement in the appointment of senior staff), their main function is as a sounding board – offering opinions which may be heard or may be ignored.

Scottish School Boards were nonetheless controversial and resisted by teachers and there was considerable alarm that they would undermine the school, the headteacher and impose a set of alien views. A 1992 study (MacBeath et al.) of Scottish School Boards reported that people were elected so as to keep the 'wrong people' off the Board, as one parent member put it 'to prevent the extremists taking over'. The report concluded that the 'extremists' never emerged and that in time the myths were punctured and fears of subversion evaporated.

Like Scotland, Danish boards have responsibility for information to parents, co-operation between home and school, approving the budget and making recommendations rather than decisions. The 1994 legislation goes somewhat further than its Scottish counterpart, however, in respect of 'laying down the principles' for the organisation of teaching, but stops considerably short of the kind of powers invested in governors in England and Wales.

FINDINGS FROM THE PROJECT

While clearly very different in constitution and power, governing bodies and School Boards were commonly seen by headteachers in our study as in danger of 'overstepping the mark', that is, going beyond what heads regarded as their legitimate role. Headteachers, teachers and parents in all three countries brought to this notion of 'overstepping', implicit assumptions about where the boundaries of expectations lay, where those of headteachers resided and where the roles of lay people stopped. These feelings were, however, overlaid in different ways in the three countries by how the governance or membership role had been centrally defined. In the English context the role of the chair of the Board was seen as 'serious managerialism':

> The chair sees it all in business terms. He is the managing director and he takes all his financial and legal responsibilities very seriously. He requires a constant supply of information.
>
> (Male headteacher)

In this example, our headteacher was not alone. Referring to her own study Rosemary Deem writes:

> ... our data also suggest that a new breed of governor, typically a co–opted business person with financial skills, legal knowledge or managerial expertise, is emerging. ... They want to know what heads are up to, they like to inspect the accounts regularly and they like to challenge what they regard as old–fashioned notions about schools being there to produce well–rounded members of society rather than future workers.
>
> (Deem, 1993, p. 211)

In one of the English schools in our study, a governing body made a decision in the head's absence which was considered by the staff to be detrimental to the school. This moved the furious head to prepare the following paper for presentation to the governing body:

Head's Expectations of the Governing Body

(1) To be always aware that they are partners, with staff, parents and the community, through the local authority, in providing the best education possible for the children who attend the school they govern.

(2) To recognise that although they have been given the ultimate responsibility and authority for the management of the school, the fundamental responsibility in practice rests with the headteacher and the staff.

(3) To recognise that their value to the partnership is directly proportional to:–

    a) their knowledge and understanding of the process of education

    b) their awareness of current issues that relate to the education system

    c) their knowledge and experience of how the school is managed and how the children are educated

    d) their relationships with all the other partners

    e) their knowledge and understanding of the children's needs.

4) To recognise that a) to e) demand a commitment of time and energy that has to be prioritised so that they are able to offer what most benefits the education of children.

A recent report by one headteachers' union (the National Association of Head Teachers, England and Wales) suggests that many of the issues emerging from our project are amplified in the national picture:

> The growth in the number of disputes with governing bodies is causing alarm, with the union reporting an increase in the number of heads under suspension ... heads were being suspended because they did not see eye–to–eye with their governing bodies and because inspections were creating a 'football–manager syndrome', where the head has to carry the can for poor reports and low league–table placings.
>
> (Rafferty, 1995, p. 1)

The report goes on to describe governors in some cases 'stepping over the mark':

> ... we do not find it acceptable for a head to return to the office to find governors who have gone through files and then make comments about the headteacher's efficiency ... governors should leave the day–to–day running of schools to the head, but those who are happy to take the lead from the head when things are going well should not then dissociate themselves when things go wrong. Delegates complained that some governors liked the power, but walked away from responsibility.
>
> (Rafferty, 1995, p. 2)

In reply to these criticisms, a representative for the National Association of Governors commented:

Governors are not just heads supporters clubs. In many cases they do not do all their tasks and the head moves into the vacuum. But where they do take on their full role, they find the head does not like it.

An English headteacher in our study, describing her experience in a London school wrote:

Some governors do not understand (or perhaps choose not to do so) that there is a separation of the strategic and operational in the running of schools. This can result in the perception that they have carte blanche to come on site without prior warning or clear purpose and attempt to involve themselves in certain matters which are palpably the province of the head.

(English headteacher)

A similar issue emerged in Denmark, although in much less dramatic terms:

The School Board has to play along with the daily life of the school. . . . Moreover I expect them to listen to the school leadership and the teacher representatives who are after all the professionals in the field. . . . There will always be issues that the School Board cannot begin to recommend on until the teachers have discussed them and reached some sort of conclusion. On the other hand, I feel it can be fruitful for the School Board to discuss things in more general terms. Then the teachers' representative and I can take these impressions with us when we go back to the Teachers' Council. But the School Board cannot just sit at a meeting and decide things straight off.

(Female head)

Sometimes it was expressed quite bluntly:

The School Board can be an inspiration to the school but it would be a mistake to allow these people, who are amateurs in educational terms, to formulate all the principles.

(Female head)

It found an echo from a School Board Chairperson in the Scottish 1992 report (MacBeath et al.):

As I see it the head will continue to make executive decisions but having to involve members, and educating members more fully in thinking and weighing up the alternatives, helping the head to make the best possible decisions.

(1992, p. 32)

The scope of influence and latitude of decision-making by the headteacher was strengthened by his or her relationship with the Education Authority. They could play a mediating role between the Board and Authority and, as one head put it, 'work in the spaces'. An illustration of this was provided by a Scottish head in our study:

The School Board meets once a month and that was one major problem I had. They were at complete loggerheads with the region and had been campaigning in the local paper over school refurbishment. I took a strong lead at the Board meetings quite deliberately and it worked. I got the refurbishment issues sorted out with an adviser and then really presented it as a fait accompli and fortunately I got away with it all right.

(Female head)

'Getting away with it' suggests a kind of political manoeuvring which headteachers were quick to admit had become a part, and a challenging part, of their job. Headteachers wanted the support of the School Board but did not want their Board to 'rock the boat' or to make life more difficult or complex for the head. Heads sometimes confessed to being 'quite manipulative' to achieve what they wanted:

Just at the point when I was appointed, the staff complained about discipline in the school to the School Board. I was aware of this coming up as an item at the School Board meeting and I was quite manipulative in preventing it being discussed by the Board. When members looked at the agenda, I introduced another item and said that it was going to take a considerable amount of time and the Board agreed to delay discussing the item on discipline until a future meeting.

(Scottish female head)

However, heads did not simply 'manipulate' their School Boards for the sake of a quiet life but usually because they were pursuing a longer-term strategy which could have been sabotaged by an open discussion at too early a stage or within an inappropriate context:

When I learnt that we were not to get a nursery despite lobbying regional headquarters, I mobilised the Board to lobby them. This stirred up a real hornets' nest but it got the school a nursery and promoted a feeling among Board members that 'they did it'. I'm now on another campaign to get the Board to take up issues of health care and diet. . . . Children in the area do have significant health care problems.

(Scottish female head)

There were instances in all three countries where, in conflicts over issues of social justice or 'equal opportunities', heads saw themselves as maintaining values intrinsic to their professionalism. In one school, where the middle-class composition of the governing body did not reflect the predominantly working-class parent body, the concerns of the middle-class parent governors (often to do with the quality of their own children's education) were not, in the head's view, always professionally defensible:

I've always felt, if it's not good enough for my child then it's not good enough for anybody's. But the value of these demanding parents is that they never allow you to forget that you have to deliver the best. They also help me to keep staff on their toes because I quote what they want. On the other hand, they do sometimes make inappropriate demands which I quietly forget. What they want is Roedean on the rates.

[Roedean is a famous fee-paying girls' school]
(Female head)

In another school, which the head described as 'racially mixed', the parents were:

> ... quite uncomfortable with some of my pronouncements about racial harassment ... you do get racists who dress up the racism in other clothes. I find that very difficult.
>
> (Male head)

As the time of interview, this head was concerned that two recently-elected parent governors were covert racists who had sought election in order to try to change the school's anti–racist stance. Again, these issues were not peculiar to our project. Rosemary Deem (1990) raises the general concern from a number of studies that

> The middle–class, white background of governors raises very real questions about the inadequate representation of working class and black or Asian groups ... largely Asian schools with mainly white governing bodies is not infrequently found and does raise issues about how, in such schools, majority working class and Asian interests are to be represented.
>
> (Deem, 1990, pp. 162–163)

In relation to gender, issues also emerged with respect to headship itself. Gerald Grace (1995) reminds us that

> ... women headteachers had encountered difficulties in the past, especially in junior and secondary schools where male-dominated governing bodies held traditional views about strong (male) dominative leadership as an essential prerequisite for headship.
>
> (Grace, 1995, p. 186)

There is some evidence from the English heads and LEA officers in our study that governors' expectations of the personal and professional qualities necessary for headship are increasingly shaped by the belief that, since running a school is comparable to running a business enterprise, then what is required is hard–nosed management of the kind to which men are often judged better suited. LEA officers, whose role in England is merely advisory, reported having 'frequently to challenge the attitudes and perspectives of governors' and one head had evidence that she was not appointed to a deputy headship earlier in her career because she had young children, a fact which was thought to cast doubt on her commitment to the job. One Scottish head assigned her failure to be selected within a particular small local authority not to gender but to parochialism amongst the School Boards:

> That was a bad time for me ... I felt there was a weight of prejudice against me, particularly from School Boards ... I was withdrawn in once instance, that I know of, by the School Board, which shouldn't have been allowed to happen. I think they are more stick in the mud in a rural authority. The parents tend to want someone who is theirs for life and lives in the community. After that experience I felt pretty let down about the whole thing.
>
> (Scottish female head)

Grace goes on to say:

> However, in the pre–reform period, once a woman was appointed as headteacher she had a relatively autonomous sphere of influence within the school. After 1988 . . . women headteachers . . . found themselves in a situation in which their conceptions of school leadership had to be made explicit and if necessary justified to male dominated governing bodies on a regular basis.
>
> (Grace, 1995)

Grace found, however, that once appointed women did not report special gender-related difficulties:

> There was no evidence in the accounts provided by the women headteachers participating in this study that these new relationships were causing any special difficulties for women. Women headteachers were as likely to report that they had 'good governors' or that they felt confident about their ability to manage or lead the governors. What cannot be predicted is how these power relations (for both men and women headteachers) will develop over time. The working relation of largely male Chairs of Governors with women headteachers on important policy issues is likely to be crucial in affecting the power sharing culture of particular schools.
>
> (Grace, 1995)

Our study confirms Grace's findings in relation to the confidence of women headteachers to manage the governors. There is also some evidence from all three countries that Grace was right to sound a sceptical note about whether women would continue to report 'no special difficulties'. One Danish female head while not experiencing 'difficulty' certainly felt irritation. In a comment which neatly summarises some twenty years of feminist research (Spender, 1980; Tannen, 1992) she said:

> I have experienced the problem after becoming Head. I hate power struggles but as leader I can't avoid them. For example if I am at a meeting it's sometimes as if the men have to sit there and push themselves forward by saying clever things without listening to what the others are saying. As the meeting develops, you begin to thinks that nothing is going to come out of it. But then you take a break for the smokers and the men go out and fix everything in a jiffy. When they come in again all the decisions are made – no matter what has been proposed already. This is just cock fighting and I refuse to waste my time on it.

Another head found herself unwillingly in the position of having to control a board member 'who just won't shut up':

> I'm really not allowed to take a back seat on the Board. I find myself in a position I wouldn't choose to be in because the Chair of the Board is not forceful. The local councillor is very forceful and wants to run it like a political meeting. He needs to be shut up and I feel I have to compensate the lack of forcefulness of the chair by trying to shut up the councillor.
>
> (Scottish female head)

This next head also experienced 'difficulty'. She had moved to a second headship and in a relatively short space of time had 'turned the school round'. As head of an infant school, she shared a governing body with the junior school situated on the same premises:

> I had to fight hard to ensure that I was properly represented on the governing body. I've had to work hard because I'm a woman. At one stage I really had to work hard because I was told by the (male) chair of governors that two chairpersons, the male head of the juniors upstairs and I, couldn't both relate to the governing body. I was to be the 'catalyst' and the other head was to be the chairperson because I was the woman. Another governor took me to British Airways for a week and I learned that different companies can report to the same governing body. I could be a chair, not a catalyst. I wrote a report and I had to do that because I was the woman. I can tell you, it really got up my back. I had a colleague in another LEA and she really supported me on that one. A lot of men aren't used to dealing with women managers.
>
> (English female head)

Difficulties were not always to do with conflict between boards and heads. Boards could sometimes be too supportive, as the 1992 Scottish study found

> They are such a nice group of people but I wish they wouldn't accede so easily everything I say. I would welcome a bit more bite, a bit more inclination to say 'Hey, wait a minute Mr. headmaster I don't think I agree with that'.
>
> (MacBeath et al., 1992, p. 28)

The theme recurred in our study. As one Scottish head put it:

> I take pains to keep them informed and they are very supportive as a result – they often don't really understand or don't know what they can do to help but they're very willing and it's up to us to let them know how they can help us.
>
> (Female head)

In Denmark a similar story emerged from the research evidence:

> We have a very good School Board with a positive attitude. They have understood that their job is to establish a framework and general principles. . . . . At a course we were on with the School Board, the School Board was encouraged to be more critical – hold preparatory meetings and so on – but they were not willing to do this. The School Board is more a supporting group and their views fit in well with the leadership.
>
> (Male head)

In England, where the penalties for 'failing' are high (and public), one head felt he had to press governors to take responsibility for his own protection:

> They would and do give me more power and control than I should have. I've gone to them and said, you should set me limits. I said I wanted a bit of protection. . . . By setting limits at least I would be able to say that I am working within the boundaries that the governors have set.
>
> (Male head).

In Denmark, a head wanted the school board more involved, not only for his own protection, but because he was committed to the kind of democratic processes that throughout the project were underlined as central to the purposes of education in preparing the next generation for their role in an advanced, complex democracy (Mahony and Moos, 1998).

> The School Board is the school's democratic alibi. It does not function as well as it might because the election procedure brings forward too few candidates. Maybe some form of direct election would be better with the parents who have been elected as the official representatives of each class.
>
> (Male head)

RELATIONSHIPS

Despite the tensions, whether expressed as conflict or complacency, heads in the project generally reported that their relationships with governors were very good. The following comment was typical:

> The school board are very supportive. They trust us. They expect high standards. They tend to treat us with respect and there is no confrontation. Their expectations are for the best educational experience and there is no evidence to suggest that isn't happening. The board will tend to back the head teacher and staff but this does not mean that they are weak and if there is something they want to raise they would do it professionally through the chair person coming to talk me.
>
> (Scottish female head).

There was a strong sense that even where there had been difficulties, the English heads felt 'lucky' with their governing bodies and, in relation to the evidence from the national level, it is not difficult to see why. In practice they gave a much higher priority to developing effective working relationships with the governors than heads from the other two countries. These good relationships were achieved by entertaining governors to lunch, either in groups or individually, by making time to meet with them informally within the school day or outside it, by being appreciative of their efforts to support the school (especially in relation to raising additional money) and by taking time to inform and 'educate' them. The end result was that relationships were often described as 'working in parallel or in harmony' to achieve the best education for the children. As we have already seen, such harmony has sometimes been a force to be reckoned with in relation to local authorities but in England, where many of the former powers of the local authority have been taken over by central government, the same potential exists:

> The Muslim community demands that the school is careful with their children and careful with their religion and culture. The legal requirement that schools conduct a daily act of Christian worship has given us a lot of problems. The school could just remain within the law but I and the governors are discussing how far we are prepared to go with what we regard as a very bad piece of

legislation. This could bring the school into conflict with the government and we have to decide how far we're prepared to go.

(Male head)

The chair of governors emerged as a key player in England and the extent to which chair and head could act together in a manner which was recognisable to the head as being 'for the good of the children' was felt to be crucial. At its best, this good relationship was seen as enhancing leadership:

When I first arrived it was a case of make the school work or it would close. The chair of governors was fantastic. I could talk things through with her completely openly and we'd work together on the best way forward. It was wonderful not being on my own with it all.

(Female head)

Michael Stark, until recently a senior policy adviser at the Department for Education and Employment (DfEE), characterises the governor as a 'friendly outsider' and 'sympathetic critic' (in Stoll and Myers, 1998). That role describes what, in practice, was a common thread in the headteacher-governor relationships in some, but not all, of the schools in England, Scotland and Denmark. The quality of relationships was seen as critical to effective Board membership as it was to successful school governance. Nonetheless, underpinning this was a significant difference in the headteacher's confidence that when it came to the crunch the authority of the head would not be undermined by the Board. As one Danish head put it 'we are employed to run this side of things'. The School Board could operate as a useful political ally or as a helpful critical friend. As one Danish female head put it 'we want the School Board to be a forum that can inject some life into things and ask all the awkward questions'. Indeed some Danish and Scottish heads expected a lot from their Boards and placed enormous demands on them:

We have a very good SB [School Board] and SA [School Association]. There are 10 School Board and 10 SA meetings a session so it's a heavy commitment but they have all done tasks and they are all looking at the departmental development plans and then coming in to visit so that's really good.

(Scottish female head)

The significance of the School Board's role in both Scotland and Denmark was not by virtue of their statutory powers but a consequence of the working relationship which they established, the leeway and responsibility allowed by headteachers and the climate of collaboration created. However, the political significance was not, in either of these two countries, equivalent to their counterpart in England – the governing bodies.

THE IMPACT ON HEADS

In Chapter 4, we wrote about parents' and School Boards' views of what constitutes the 'good' headteacher. We also asked the heads what they thought the School Boards expected of them. Whether or not the beliefs, or putative beliefs, actually bore any relationship to reality was in a sense inconsequential as they would still exert a powerful influence on headteachers and leadership more generally.

Danish heads thought that the School Board expected them to be 'promoting, creative, development-orientated and conflict-solving'. The Scottish heads said they 'expect me to keep them informed' and to achieve 'high standards'. In interviews with Scottish and Danish heads the question about expectations of Boards was often ignored in favour of a more discursive treatment of the role of the Board. This was not the case for the English heads who were acutely conscious of their governing body's expectations of them. Their accounts of those expectations were detailed and remarkably consistent. Some of them were, for example: 'to run the school efficiently (within a tight budget)'; 'to be kept fully informed'; 'to run a well disciplined, happy and well motivated school' and 'a school where all the partners work in some sort of harmony'.

In short, in the view of heads, governors expected them to manage the school so that there were 'no problems with children, staff, parents or money'. Put together like this, these expectations can be clearly seen to contain three contradictory discourses: the 'professional'; the 'community' and the 'business or entrepreneurial'. These three, argues Ball (1994), construct 'new headship'. The contradictions between them derive from fundamentally different conceptions of the nature and purpose of education (Sidgwick et al., 1994) and the tensions between them were not lost on those heads who, during our project, faced the prospect of maintaining 'a happy school' within a context of managing staff redundancy.

A number of English heads reported that the expectations of the governors had changed over time. These were seen as a developing response to their new powers and responsibilities and having come to terms with what these involved. They were also a response to improvements in the school's performance or, more typically, because the heads had coaxed them into taking a more active part. No head thought that her or his expectations had been shaped by the governors. On the contrary, they believed that they were leading the school and that governors were content to follow their professional guidance, once their confidence and trust had been won.

There was one area, however, where governors were clearly perceived as having an impact on the English heads. That was in relation to their next career move. The view was often expressed that there is a 'sell by date' to headship and in the past it was not uncommon for heads to move on to take up appointments in university Departments of Education or into the Inspectorate. Both have been 'reformed' in England within wider transformations in the public sector and the opportunities which were once attractive to heads have either ceased to be so or no longer exist. What heads do once they have passed their 'sell by date' in a particular school was a concern raised a number of times. For some heads the obvious answer was a second headship. However, the spectre of a 'bad' governing body and the fact that 'the governors are paying me way over the odds to keep me', as one male headteacher put it, were both factors that dissuaded heads from moving to another school.

Three tentative conclusions can be reached about the English situation as it existed for the duration of the project. First, while day to day relationships with the governors were generally reported as supportive, one bad experience, the appointment of new (and unknown) governors, knowledge of difficulties in another school and the lack of clarity in the respective roles and responsibilities of heads and governing bodies, all created uncertainty and anxiety for heads and operated to keep them 'up to the wire' even while relationships were harmonious.

Second, good relationships were only achieved by dint of a great deal of hard work, time, social skill and 'politics with a small p'. The question must be asked whether the energy and other resources which went into establishing and maintaining the trust and confidence of the governors enhanced or diverted the work of the head and whether there are other ways of facilitating what is surely the legitimate democratic involvement of the community in the governance of schools.

Third, as things currently stand, contradiction is built into the role of heads and the expectations of them. Precisely how these contradictions are experienced on a day-by-day basis, and how they articulate with the technical aspects of the head's work, are matters which are discussed elsewhere in the book.

Underpinning all the considerations to do with school governance, whether in Denmark, England or Scotland, are issues of power: who has it, how it is maintained, how it is used and for whose benefit. Although the policy context at the macro level may shape the parameters of how schools operate, it is at the micro level of the school itself that policy is translated into practice. The head is undoubtedly a highly significant person in this process and may use or misuse her or his considerable power in pursuit of particular values, constrained to a greater or lesser extent by the parameters laid down by central government (Mahony and Moos, 1998). For all their reservations about the rights of 'amateurs' to be involved in the running of schools, devolved governance can provide heads with a 'democratic alibi' as much as it can challenge them to justify their professional values or to move beyond the tokenistic acceptance of a rhetoric of local accountability. The evidence from our project might even suggest the reverse of Ball's view that 'uncertainty, trials of strength, manipulation and conflict . . . hardly seem the basis for . . . clear and effective school leadership' (1994, p. 88). It could be that effective school leadership is in part defined in relation to the ability of heads to incorporate and utilise such dimensions in pursuit of their ultimate goals.

REFERENCES

Ball, S. (1994) *Education Reform: A Critical and Post–Structural Approach,* Open University Press, Buckingham.

Deem, R. (1990) The reform of school governing bodies: the power of the consumer over the producer?, in M. Flude and M. Hammer (eds.)*The Education Reform Act 1988: Its Origins and Implications,* Falmer, London.

Deem, R. (1993) 'Educational reform and school governing bodies in England 1986–92: old dogs, new tricks or new dogs, new tricks?, in M. Preedy (ed.) *Managing the Effective School,* Paul Chapman, London.

Grace G. (1995) *School Leadership: Beyond Education Management,* Falmer, London.

MacBeath, J., Thomson, W. and McCaig, E. (1992) *Making School Boards Work,* Scottish Education Department, Jordanhill College, Glasgow.

Mahony, P. and Moos, L. (1998) Central and local expectations of school leadership. Paper given to the Effective Leadership in a Time of Change Conference, Lancashire LEA, 8 January.

Rafferty, F. (1995) Football governors attacked by head, *Times Educational Supplement,* 2 June.

Sidgwick, S., Mahony, P. and Hextall, I. (1994) A gap in the market?, *British Journal of Sociology of Education,* Vol. 15, no. 4, pp. 467–479.

Spender, D. (1980) *Man-made Language,* Routledge and Kegan Paul, London.

Stoll, L. and Myers, K. (1998) *No Quick Fixes,* Falmer, London.

Tannen, D. (1992) *You just don't understand: women and men in conversation,* Virago, London.

8

Ethical Challenges in School Leadership

Neil Dempster and Pat Mahony

INTRODUCTION

In Chapters 5 and 6, dilemmas faced by principals in making leadership and management decisions in their schools were discussed. Although our study was not focused specifically on the ethics of leadership, they impinged upon it during the course of the research because of what principals were saying. This chapter examines in more depth the issues which touched on ethical decision-making. It then presents data gathered by different methods, including examples of the ethical dilemmas principals face in the everyday operation of self-managed schools. This is followed by a discussion of what we learned from the limited amount of data available. The chapter concludes with ideas for further research needing to be done if principals are to be better informed when they meet troublesome ethical issues in the future.

INTEREST IN ETHICAL DECISION-MAKING

During the study, interest in how headteachers approach and cope with ethical issues arose from four sources – case study interviews, literature on educational leadership, ideas about leading in devolving systems and concerns over the influence of market theory in education.

First, the case study interviews with headteachers in England, Scotland, Denmark and Australia revealed a major preoccupation with the ethical dimensions of leadership. From conversations about how principles of leadership were translated into action, it emerged that in quite self-conscious ways headteachers relied on their values to guide their actions. They even used negative experiences such as conflicts amongst staff to stamp their values on the school. There was also evidence that people weighed up the merits of taking one course of action rather than another, or of not acting at all in terms of their ethical consequences for different groups or individuals. In a number of cases, dilemmas were posed when it was thought that a course of action would produce both positive and negative outcomes or when a positive outcome for one group was perceived to be at the expense of another. Discomfort was also expressed, particularly by English heads, at some of the difficult decisions to be made as to how best to use decreasing budgets. For example, should resources be targeted at those children who might improve the school's position in the league tables or at those with learning or behavioural difficulties?

This concern with ethical issues was always at a practical level, raised by example rather than by the domains from which most ethical issues originate. However, there was sufficient information to indicate that often the matter of children's entitlement conflicted with financial constraints. Principles of equality conflicted with those of excellence and questions of freedom conflicted with control in the school and how students and staff ought to be treated.

The second source of interest was the literature on educational leadership in which increasing attention is being paid to the ethical dimensions of the head's role (Foster, 1989; Bottery, 1993; Hodgkinson, 1993; Grace, 1995). In studies of educational administration, there is general agreement that leadership is values driven, and therefore leaders should be cognisant of, and act appropriately, when faced with the many ethical problems presented by schooling (Evers et al., 1992; Office of Education Research and Improvement, 1989; Sergiovanni, 1992; Starratt, 1991). This is not surprising since there are very strong arguments to support the view that all professions, including teaching, possess a moral dimension (Fenstermacher, 1990).

Primary amongst these arguments is the notion that the practitioner engages with an element of the client's life in order to bring about changes that are in the client's best interests. So, for example, the surgeon alters the physical status of patients by operating on their bodies in order to improve their health; the psychologist aims to bring about improvements in a client's mental health by means of specialised conversations; and the school principal is concerned with providing experiences to school children that will help transform them into adults capable of living 'good lives'. All these instances are characterised by the idea that normative concerns govern the practice of professionals. That is, professionals work towards making things better. There are, however, always contestable judgements to be made about what is involved in living a better life, for both client and professional. And because it is not always clear just what the best action is, engagement with normative complexity is an important and enduring feature of professional life. Other published research (Walker, 1995) suggests that school leaders find these normative complexities a major concern, struggling with the competing interests of participants in schooling as well as their own sense of personal integrity. Recent work by Dymock (1996) highlights the range of dilemmas faced by heads. These he classifies in two ways – states of mind and specific dilemmas. The former includes competing views about leadership, role and position. The latter include competing views about the purposes and functions of schooling, school structures and processes, curriculum, teaching, learning and resources. Dymock (1996) argues that the head's involvement in dealing with dilemmas has increased over recent years as education systems have restructured.

The third source of our interest concerns this very matter, that is, restructuring and the devolution of authority and responsibility to school sites which has brought increasing powers to the school principal. Even in systems where the head's power is supposedly constrained by the formal and legal powers of a governing body, as in England or Victoria, Australia for example, we have found that governors are often reluctant or unable to undertake their responsibilities, even if heads are keen for them to do so. Other studies have revealed that governors often delegate their responsibilities so that in real terms the balance of power and control remains firmly with the head (Burgess et al., 1992; Maychell, 1994, Levacic and Glover, 1994). These findings are reinforced by the work of Chrispeels (1992) and Highett (1992) who claim that principals are sometimes more concerned with the form than the substance of sharing power. Genuine parent and community involvement in school leadership and management can be circumscribed by heads, often in collusion with staff and 'insider' parents. The picture that emerges from these kinds of studies is one of the retention of power by the head, aided by compliant or apathetic parents and teachers. When this is the case, heads act at best on a 'heroic' model of leadership, at worst on an autocratic model.

These findings say nothing of the ethical questions tied up in the leadership model used consciously or unconsciously by heads. The 'states of mind' dilemmas identified by Dymock (1996, pp. 145, 146) carry with them the kind of ethical questions to which we refer. We have generated several examples from his list to illustrate the point.

- Should I regard myself as head of a self-managing school or should I see myself as a line agent in a system's chain of control?
- Should I be a proactive leader of the school community or should I be reactive to the school community?
- Should I be the initiator of change or should I be the gatekeeper, the preserver of tradition?
- Should I emphasise evaluation, sanction and accountability in my leadership or should I focus on support, improvement and celebration?

If it is accepted that leadership is a relational concept which logically implies the existence of at least one other person who is led or who follows, then the ethical debate is about how power ought to be exercised in an organisation and by whom. As Dymock's (1996) research shows, heads themselves struggle with this debate with some contending that the main function of leaders is to create followers (Busher and Saran, 1994).

> What ought to be a matter for debate becomes instead structured into language with the danger that we become so enamoured of this cult of heroic leadership that we fail to see its obvious contradictions. For example, in the name of empowering the workers, we actually reinforce hierarchy. So-called empowerment becomes the empty gift of the bosses, who remain firmly in charge.
>
> (Mintzberg, 1996, p. 80)

The model of heroic leadership and derivatives of it have often been rejected by modern management theorists as inappropriate in business, industry and commerce (Mintzberg, 1996). We argue that if it is applied in education, it places the school leader in the untenable position of sole moral arbiter in ethical issues which arise in the school. The results of our study show that English heads are expected to be more like the heroic leader than are their Scottish, Australian and Danish counterparts but in all countries, the educational leadership rhetoric calls for greater power sharing amongst all stakeholders (Rallis, 1988; Fullan, 1991).

The fourth source of our interest lies in governments applying economic rationalist principles and market-oriented solutions to the provision of services in ways, as we have explained earlier, which may not be as appropriate in the provision of education as they are in the sale of products for profit. As Robertson asserts:

> It takes little effort to demonstrate that while the marketplace has been an exceedingly effective mechanism to generate wealth, on the whole its success has been achieved because of, not despite its lack of a moral core. This is not a character flaw but a characteristic. Markets are not moral; they are necessarily preoccupied with self-interest and advantage and as such, are unfit arbiters of what constitutes our collective well-being.
>
> (Robertson, 1997, p. 3)

Robertson expands her argument to show how the application of market theory to the provision of a public good, such as education, places school leaders in an increasingly difficult ethical position as they attempt to manage their 'businesses' efficiently and effectively. Boylett and Finlay go further than this by suggesting that in the past

> public sector management's prime objective was recognised as a moral absolute to 'do good' rather than prioritising objectives in relative economic terms. But the changes imposed by parental choice and outcome-led performance measurement of school efficiency and effectiveness have turned the philosophy of school management on its head.
>
> (Boylett and Finlay, 1996, p. 34)

The points we have described in this brief review of some of the relevant literature, and the circumstances created by contemporary approaches to public sector management, have marked out a new set of conditions in which heads must exercise leadership. When deregulation has been pursued, when decision-making has been localised, when safety-nets and supports have been withdrawn, when policy parameters dictate particular courses of action irrespective of context – all of these circumstances add to the complexity of the climate in which decisions must be made at school level. The challenge now lies on at least two fronts, first, settling the question of what kind of leadership should prevail in these circumstances by articulating the professional values that underpin the head's role; and second, developing consistent approaches to deal with the normative complexity around the ethical dilemmas arising in the course of everyday school life.

ETHICAL DILEMMAS FACED BY PRINCIPALS

Ethical dilemmas arise when a course of action must be chosen from among a number of options, some of which may be inappropriate or wrong when judged from the standpoint of particular values and moral principles. Rather than enter into a philosophical discussion, we describe a number of dilemmas that the principals in our study reported or which were raised during discussions with them. These practical examples enable us to see the nature of a dilemma and the implicit professional ethics and moral principles. The examples are presented from two perspectives, where the origin of the dilemma is primarily external or internal to the school.

DILEMMAS WITH EXTERNAL ORIGINS

Dilemma Number One

The first dilemma is the result of the mendicant financial status of most schools. They are dependent on government allocations and it is well known that these change over time. Schools have almost no control over their annual operating grants and over recent years many have had to manage with reduced budgets because of government cutbacks.

> With a reducing budget this year, there is considerable tension when it comes to staffing. I can't save very much on minor things like resources and equipment in one school year so I've got to cut the salary bill. The trouble is I've got a really good staff who are working incredibly hard. How can I turn around and say to one of them: 'Sorry, we can't afford to pay you any more'? And which one do I say it to?

Dilemma Number Two

The second dilemma concerns school closures. These take time. They are sometimes preceded by classification as 'failing schools' as in England or they are known on the 'grapevine' to be on a government list for closure because of falling numbers. Whatever the case, it soon becomes common knowledge that a school is under pressure from its authorities. When surrounding schools have the capacity to gain additional funds by increasing their enrolments, they feel under pressure to do so.

> When a neighbouring school is known to have a threatened future, should I drop leaflets in its locality with details about my own school? Do I openly advertise that I will accept transfers from students already on courses? Do I market my school in the hope of getting extra students knowing that the other school may suffer as a result?

Dilemma Number Three

The third dilemma is about income generation and the role of sponsorship in schools. It is commonplace these days for large companies to enter into partnerships with individuals or organisations through sponsorships which attempt to gain wider exposure for particular products in an increasingly competitive marketplace. Schools have always been the home of a youth market and it comes as no surprise that companies would be interested in advertising or sponsorship deals with them.

I have been approached by a large national company which wishes to place screen saver messages about its products on all of our computers. We are a large secondary school and we have over a hundred computers available for student use. The company markets itself directly to adolescents and its screen saver message advertises its products directly to computer users whenever they are not actively working on tasks of their own. There is a considerable licence fee payable to the school if I agree. We are always in need of extra funds yet I am uncomfortable with the idea that students would be exposed to single product advertising in a manner which tacitly seems to endorse those products.

Dilemma Number Four

Competition among government schools has begun to emerge as a consequence of funding formulae which link income directly to student numbers. When enrolments fall, income goes down, creating a roll-on effect into curriculum, staffing, equipment and facilities. Schools are increasingly having to develop strategies to ensure that their enrolments are maintained or even enhanced if they want additional funds for innovatory programmes.

Three years ago we made a strategic change in our school's curriculum. We introduced electronics and technology courses and linked these with our major efforts in music and theatre. These changes have increased demand and we are holding our own in enrolments against the three other high schools in our area. However, I have noticed that courses in family studies and home economics are failing to attract the numbers of students they did in the past. These subjects require a great amount of space and expensive equipment, especially for training kitchens. We could well do with the extra space and extra funds to expand our technology centre and our most popular courses. Such an expansion would also consolidate our curriculum specialisations which really help me in marketing the school.

Dilemma Number Five

Governments during the late 1980s and early 1990s shifted the educational policy focus from concern for inputs to concern for outcomes. Measures of student achievement have since become critical yardsticks of how parents and members of the public make judgements about a school's performance.

We know that we lose quite a number of good local students to other schools in the city because their parents see our results in the League Tables – results which, because of our student base, place us in the bottom third of the list. The Council wants to set aside some money from this year's budget to offer ten students from our local primary schools a substantial bursary to attend this school. This money would be taken from the little we have at our discretion and I am troubled by the 'gung-ho' manner in which Council members are discussing a decision which they say will lift our standards.

DILEMMAS WITH INTERNAL ORIGINS

Dilemma Number Six

Parents are increasingly critical of teachers and their teaching methods and they often take their complaints directly to the school. Principals find themselves having to respond to these complaints quickly but within what is considered 'due process', that is, procedures resulting from industrial action by unions and associations which have the force of law.

We've got a teacher who gets constant complaints from parents and students. We've given him a lot of professional development and gone through all the business of setting targets etc. He has met some of them but not others so it still isn't clear cut. Should I now make his life a misery to get rid of him?

Dilemma Number Seven

There are certain social problems like the use of drugs by young people which are viewed with absolute disquiet by parents and teachers alike. Drug education programmes are always controversial but more troublesome is an exposé of drugs in schools by a sensationalist press.

I dare not admit publicly that we've got a drugs problem in the school in case it damages our reputation. This would mean that we would lose pupils and therefore funding. Yet, if I don't admit it we can't undertake a concerted effort with the parents and support services to tackle it properly. Neither do I want to permanently exclude the offending students as other schools have done even though I know that would improve our reputation.

Dilemma Number Eight

Principals are required to appraise teachers formally in many countries. However, given the 'closed door' nature of classroom work and the view by many that teachers are professionals who should carry out their work unsupervised, it is often very difficult for principals to gain a firsthand view of the practice of their teachers.

There is an ethical issue in going into classrooms to find out what is going on and whether it is good enough and making teachers insecure by having them feel that I am spying on them. I'm not sure what position I should be adopting.

Dilemma Number Nine

The average age of teachers has increased in all four countries included in the leadership study. For example, in Australia, the average which was 37.6 years in 1990 (Logan et al., 1990) is now over forty. This figure is higher in the United Kingdom and Denmark. Financial problems can accompany the fact that older teachers command higher salaries than do new appointees.

> I lead a small school with fifteen teachers. Twelve of them have been at the school for over ten years and of this group, nine are at the top of their salary scales. I am under pressure from parents to improve the fabric of the school but with over ninety per cent of our budget spent on salaries, I am being forced to think about reducing the salary bill. I could do this by offering redundancies to a number of the most expensive teachers and by replacing them with beginning teachers who are cheaper. This would free up some money over the longer term but I worry about how much the quality of what we do would be affected.

Dilemma Number Ten

Government schools have traditionally opened their doors to all in England, Scotland, Denmark and Australia. As a result, many enrol students from a diverse range of cultural backgrounds. In these schools, the participation of parents, though a policy imperative, presents difficulties.

> Our School Council and its sub-committees, do not contain anyone whose first language is not English (Danish), yet we have many Eastern European and Asian families whose children attend the school. Even though most of our pupils are from the mainstream or home culture, I feel that we are further marginalising our ethnic groups by seeming to exclude them from the forums that make decisions about the school. However, members of the Council are either appointed or elected and these processes reinforce what has always happened. The Chair of the Council isn't concerned about this at all.

The examples we have described above capture the spirit of the dilemmas headteachers encounter. In their discussions with us, heads reported that they often felt alone, cast in the role of arbiter or mediator relying on personal values and professional ethics to find a morally defensible decision. Such a role runs against the tide of collaborative approaches to leadership and the sharing of power in decision-making which, as we have argued, are ethical issues in their own right.

To sum up, dilemmas involve people, resources and power and more often than not, all three are implicated in particular courses of action chosen. If Giddens's (1984) definition of power is accepted as the exercise of control over people and resources, then it is clear that ethical decision-making is about the head's use of power. This goes a long way towards explaining why the model of leadership employed by the head is so critical in the way a school is run and in the resolution of competing demands.

DATA FROM THE STUDY

This part of the chapter presents and discusses data gained about ethics and leadership from two different approaches used during the study – the first with transcripts from our Australian work, the second in workshops with English, Scottish and Danish heads.

The Australian Transcripts

As we indicated at the outset, our interest in this topic was raised partly because heads spoke of it in interviews. In the Australian work, transcripts from twelve such interviews were subjected to a second detailed analysis in which explicit values informing the head's actions, and the kinds of decisions in which they reported involvement, were noted. This analysis, a summary of which we present here, though far from extensive, suggests that concerns with ethical behaviour, personal values positions and consistency in decision-making are perceived by heads to be significant in carrying out their duties.

In reanalysing the twelve transcripts, we concentrated on isolating situations in which decisions were described by principals. Next, we looked for text to show the meanings attached to these situations and then we identified a value or values that seemed to be implicated in what the principal had said. The following examples illustrate the technique we used:

Situations	Meanings	Values
My second school was a poor, low socio-economic, inner city school with a number of big ethnic groups. There was a very big range of rich and poor in the community but I never experienced the bitterness there that I did in my previous, much wealthier school. In my second school, I had a very rich experience spanning ten years and it gave me back my confidence in people who are better off than others. These well-off people had made a choice to be part of a school	Good relationships are possible among different groups in society. However, it takes confidence to live with a multicultural community on all sides. It is so easy for the well-off to choose to live in other communities but they lose any idea of how affirming close relationships with all sorts of people in society can be.	multiculturalism equity social justice

community with a multicultural mix.

At a recent swimming carnival, I was walking down the concourse when I saw one of my students walking by. She had new swimmers on, so I said, 'Come over here Jo'. She stopped, she looked behind and around her to see what was happening and then she came over to me and said, 'Yes. What's wrong?' I said, 'Nothing'. And she said, 'Well, I thought if you wanted to speak to me, there must be something wrong'. 'How dreadful', I thought.

If you are out there mixing with the students more and more, you will get fewer and fewer situations where you have to be hard or be viewed as hard. When I hear people say, 'Oh, we couldn't come to your office because you're the principal', I think, 'Where on earth did you get that feeling? Where have I gone wrong?'

empathy
accessibility

I was trying to explain to one of my adolescent students that his views were not necessarily the only right views and that a little bit of give and take was necessary if he was going to avoid confrontations with other boys in the future. A bit of humility from time to time would not hurt, I said. When you talk to 14 year-olds about this and you spend 35 minutes doing it, you are working bloody hard I can tell you.

I have an expectation of myself that I should be dispassionate and impartial when dealing with students in trouble. I also would like to think that I am intellectually humble, that is, I will be open to ideas other than my own, because if you are not humble, you cannot be receptive.

intellectual humility

Other values carried in principals' descriptions included concern for excellence but high regard for ability and effort, self-determination yet social responsibility, altruism tempered by responsiveness to practicalities, sensitivity to context in pursuing bold visions, intellectual achievement but the celebration of all success, consultation and collaboration while seeking consensus, building a sense of individual and community empowerment with trust amongst all parties. These values were not articulated in any systematic way, nor do they make an exemplary list of what lies at the heart of good school leadership and management. However, the situations principals have described indicate how much personal stake there is in their everyday actions while highlighting implicit values, tensions and a concern for consistency in dealing with members of the school community.

THE WORKSHOPS WITH ENGLISH, SCOTTISH AND DANISH HEADS

In this approach, Danish, English and Scottish heads, organised in their national groups, were asked to discuss six moral dilemmas. They were asked to focus on what should be done in response to the dilemmas and then to tease out the principles underpinning their answers. Five of the dilemmas used are included in the ten described in the previous section – numbers one, two, six, seven and eight. Three of these dilemmas were drawn directly from transcripts of head's interviews (one from each country) and two from the literature on leadership. The sixth was left blank as an open invitation for the heads to identify a dilemma for themselves. It is important to note that in planning and preparing the workshop, researchers from all three countries had taken particular care to check that the selection of dilemmas was appropriate for consideration by heads in their countries. The outcomes from the heads' participation in this exercise were unexpected.

The Danish heads crossed through with heavy emphasis the majority of the dilemmas reproduced in their workshop materials and they left blank the space provided for the sixth dilemma. Their discussion concentrated mainly on denying (sometimes angrily) that such dilemmas existed or could exist. This denial was viewed with scepticism by the Danish researchers who felt that there was adequate evidence to indicate that dilemmas such as the ones addressed were being encountered in Folkeskoles.

The English heads responded to the five dilemmas provided but in a way which seemed to belie the personal angst which had been expressed in the privacy of their interviews. Any sense of dilemma disappeared to be replaced by the proposal of clear courses of action underpinned by strongly expressed moral principles. The blank space for a sixth dilemma remained untouched.

The Scottish heads also addressed the five written dilemmas and here a sense of the struggles between the demands of the market and the survival of the school became evident. In the words of one head:

We have a real concern about the weakening of collaborative structures. We're a public service and if we're not then we all lose out in the long run.

Even so, the sense of dilemma was weak and the space for the recording of a dilemma of their own was again left blank.

In a subsequent meeting, English heads were asked why the activity had not provided an opportunity to talk about their concerns and why it had not been successful in enabling them to reveal what their concerns really were. A number of suggestions were made which ranged from:

I'm not going to reveal in public how vile I can be

to:

We know what to do. It's the pain and suffering of others, the people bit of it which is awful. What am I going to do isn't necessarily a request for a solution. It's a cry for understanding – look how awful this is for me.

There are important lessons to be drawn from the workshop which, to put it bluntly, simply did not work as a means of examining how heads go about resolving competing demands ethically. It was too public and heads felt exposed and pressured to present themselves in any way other than morally virtuous. In addition, this workshop approach suffered from being an artificial 'one-off' activity rather than part of a much longer discussion about ethical leadership backed by a broader evidence base located within a wider literature. The examples used were also distanced from the immediate problems heads were experiencing while being close enough to smack of a 'moral test'.

More successful than heads' responses to the five dilemmas, at least in terms of their engagement, was the development of a set of principles which they felt ought to underpin headteachers' actions. These principles concerned children, staff and external relations.

Children

- children come first;
- children have a right to a good education and to be safe; and
- their health and welfare are priorities.

Staff

- decisions about staff should be consistent and based on clear criteria;
- staff ought not to have to carry colleagues;
- it is the head's responsibility to deal with staffing situations;
- one ought not be manipulative;
- staff have a right and a duty to be involved in improving quality; and
- the head has a right and a duty to know what is going on.

External relations

- do as you would be done by in relation to other schools;
- heads should recognise their wider responsibility to the community; and

- heads should recognise the external context and lobby or galvanise political support if necessary.

These principles, produced through workshop discussions, need rigorous scrutiny and assessment in practical circumstances if they are to be more than a bland set of pieties to which even ruthless, autocratic and morally reprehensible heads might subscribe. The devil lies in the detail, first in how consistently principles such as these can be applied in resolving real life dilemmas; second, in what is meant by such terms as a 'good education', 'health' and 'welfare' for children. Such issues have been at the very heart of moral philosophy over the past two thousand years and they mark merely the continuation of debates which, in our view, are necessary in the professional development of heads.

FURTHER RESEARCH

It is clear from the preceding discussion that our study only 'scratched the surface' of what looms as a very difficult field of professional activity for school leaders. We have encountered, or had reported to us, a whole range of dilemmas requiring ethical decisions by heads. These include issues of student selection, streaming, exclusion, the teacher age profile, youth versus experience, teaching competence, continuity of employment, parent inclusion and marginalisation, income generation, sponsorship, fees, scholarships, marketable curriculum specialisations, advertising and poaching, to name but a few. It is our view that heads need access to a substantial knowledge base about the management of this terrain and that knowledge base can only be built through further empirical research into the professional values on which heads base their leadership; morally defensible decision-making processes consistent with those leadership values; and the types of ethical solutions available when difficult dilemmas are encountered.

Dymock (1996) supports this view, particularly with respect to the use of the dilemma as a means to enhancing our understanding. Without this kind of applied research and the accompanying development of theory on ethical models of leadership in today's and tomorrow's schools, much of the experience that heads gain as they carry out their duties will remain lost to colleagues who might benefit from it. This scholarly work is essential because whether we like it or not, under new public sector management, there are emerging irreconcilable goals for schooling. On the one hand there are those who are pushing schools to operate like businesses and to pursue the educational equivalent of profit maximisation. On the other hand, schools are ultimately concerned with the development of students who are not only employable, but also autonomous, responsible, moral individuals who are effective members of society (Association of Teachers of English of Nova Scotia, 1996). Heads who are able to model moral leadership in the way they run their schools are more likely, in our view, to concentrate on the ultimate goal of schooling, even though they are constantly under pressure to do otherwise.

REFERENCES

Association of Teachers of English of Nova Scotia [ATENS] (1996) *A Shared Vision: A Report on Education-Business Partnerships*, Nova Scotia Teachers' Union, Halifax.

Bottery, M. (1993) *The Ethics of Educational Management*, Cassell, London.

Boylett, I., and Finlay, D. (1996) Corporate governance and the school headteacher, *Public Money and Management*, April–June, pp. 31–38.

Burgess, R. G. et al. (1992) *Thematic Report and Case Studies*, Sheffield City Council, Sheffield.

Busher, H., and Saran, R. (1994) Towards a model of school leadership, *Educational Management and Administration*, Vol. 22, no. 1, pp. 5–13.

Chrispeels, J. (1992) *Purposeful Restructuring: Creating a Culture for Learning and Achieving in Elementary Schools*, Falmer, Lewes.

Dymock, C. (1996) Dilemmas for school leaders and administrators in restructuring, in K. Leithwood, J. Chapman, D. Corson, P. Hallinger and A. Hart, (eds.) *International Handbook of Educational Leadership, and Administration*, Vol. 1, Kluwer, Dordrecht.

Evers, C. W., Duigan, P. A. and MacPherson, R. J. S. (1992) Ethics and ethical theory, in P. A. Duigan and R. J. S. MacPherson (eds.) *Educative Leadership: a practical theory for new administrators and managers*, Falmer Press, London.

Fenstermacher, G. D. (1990) Moral considerations on teaching as a profession, in J. J. Good, R. Soder, and K. A. Sirotnic, (eds.) *Moral Dimensions of Teaching*, Jossey-Bass, San Francisco.

Foster, W. (1989) Towards a critical practice of leadership, in J. Smyth (ed.) *Critical Perspectives on Educational Leadership*, Falmer, London.

Fullan, M. G. (1991) *The New Meaning of Educational Change*, Cassell, London.

Giddens, A. (1984) *The Constitution of Society*, Polity Press, Cambridge.

Grace, G. (1995) *School Leadership: Beyond Education Management*, Falmer, London.

Highett, N. (1992) School development planning in Queensland, *Unicorn*, Vol. 18, no. 2, pp. 17–24.

Hodgkinson, C. (1993) *The Philosophy of Leadership*, Basil Blackwell, Oxford.

Levacic, R and Glover, D. (1994) *OFSTED: Assessment of Schools' Efficiency*, Open University Press, Milton Keynes.

Logan, L., Dempster, N., Berkeley, G., Chant, D., Howell, M. and Warry, M. (1990) *Teachers in Australian Schools: A 1989 Profile*, The Australian College of Education, Canberra.

Maychell, K. (1994) *Counting the Cost: The Impact of LMS on Schools' Patterns of Spending*, NFER, Slough.

Mintzberg, H. (1996) Managing government: governing management, *Harvard Business Review*, May–June, pp. 75–83.

Office of Education Research and Improvement (1989) Ethics and the school administrator, the best of ERIC, *Educational Management*, No. 100, Washington DC.

Rallis, S. F. et al. (1995) *Dynamic Teachers: leaders of change*, Corwin Press, Thousand Oaks, California.

Robertson, H. (1997) Partnerships in public education or McSchool meets McWorld. Paper given at the 17th Annual Seminar of the International Society of Teacher Education, Brock University, Canada, May.

Sergiovanni, T. J. (1992) *Moral Leadership: Getting to the Heart of School Improvement*, Jossey-Bass, San Francisco.

Starratt, R. J. (1991) *Building an ethical school: a theory for practice in Educational Leadership*, Falmer Press, London.

Walker, K. D. (1995) Perceptions of ethical problems among senior educational leaders, *Journal of School Leadership*, Vol. 5, no. 6, pp. 532–63.

9

Effective Leaders and Effective Schools

Kathryn Riley and John MacBeath

Effective schools can be good schools, and good schools must be effective
schools – but the two are not necessarily the same.
(Carl Glickman, 1987, quoted in Silver, 1994, p. 102)

INTRODUCTION

When we first began our project on school leadership, we adopted the title
'Effective School Leadership in a Time of Change'. In choosing such
terminology, we wanted to reflect the shifting grounds of school leadership
and the rapid economic and social changes, in what is increasingly a
globalised context. The juxtaposition of the two words 'effective' and
'leadership' signified the growing emphasis on school outcome measures and
the growing acceptance of leadership as a key constituent in the 'effective'
school (Sammons et al., 1995).

In the four countries in our study, leadership had become an urgent policy
issue, an integral component of the drive for more effective schools, raised
achievement and public accountability. From a policy-maker's perspective,
'effective leadership' could perhaps be seen as holding the key to resolving
many of the problems which appeared to be facing schools, but what
assumptions lay behind that notion? Were there some generic and resilient
features of effective leadership impervious to changes in time and place? Were
there common competencies? Could leadership be constructed from a set of
component parts?

The starting point for our research was how school leaders themselves
conceptualised 'leadership', the expectations which they brought to that role
and how their expectations meshed with those of other stakeholders.
Differences in context and culture came to the surface because of the
international nature of our project, and sharpened our awareness of how
school leadership is shaped by socio-economic and political factors. It
returned us persistently to the point where cultural history meets
contemporary politics, and where globalisation confronts national identity
(MacBeath et al., 1996).

As an international research team, we were a motley crew, and our thinking about leadership derived from many perspectives and disciplines including sociology, philosophy, psychology, policy and management. The project itself had emerged through a common interest in school effectiveness and improvement; we knew the literature; we were engaged in projects in the field; we attended conferences with the school effectiveness theme; and we accepted the assumption inherent in the school effectiveness literature that schools could make a difference. Nevertheless, we shared some unease about what 'making a difference' meant and how it was measured. We were uncomfortable with the term 'effective' being appropriated to refer only to measured differences on student attainment between school A and school B. We were also interested in the questions which this raised about the relationship between leadership as 'effective' and schools as 'effective'.

Exploring leadership, effective schools and their inter-relationship raised, for us, three fundamental questions:

- What do we understand by the terms 'effective' and 'good'?
- What is the relationship between effective leaders and effective schools?
- Are there models (of effective schools and effective leadership) which can be legitimately transferred?

These are the questions which we raise and attempt to answer in this chapter.

THE 'EFFECTIVE' HEADTEACHER RECIPE

The growing internationalisation of education has meant that the language of school effectiveness has become common currency amongst researchers, and has shaped the thinking of policy-makers. The climate of global competitiveness which now characterises much national thinking about education is receptive to the 'quick-fix' in school effectiveness, as in other areas. 'Policy borrowing', reinforced by a belief that education models are transferable, regardless of context, is becoming standard practice.

Effective leadership in a time of change is, therefore, a bold title. It appears to promise an answer or perhaps even a recipe, but if we have learned one thing from our study it is that there is no one package for school leadership, no one model to be learned and applied in unrefined forms, for all schools, in all contexts – no all-purpose recipe. Nonetheless, there are clearly some common ingredients and the collaborative sharing of thinking and practice in which our study was rooted provided the opportunity for participating heads to look at the critical mix. From working alongside thirty heads from three countries (and then forty as the Australian heads joined the study), it became increasingly obvious that successful school leaders do not learn how to 'do' leadership and then stick to set patterns and ways of doing things along a prescribed set of known rules. They are willing to change in response to new sets of circumstances – and to the differing needs of children, young people and teachers – and they are often rule breakers.

Notions of leadership are profoundly value-laden. They relate to national purposes, local context, as well as the skills and attributes of individuals, and the demands and expectations of school communities. Demands and expectations change over time. By and large, the role of the school principal, or headteacher of a decade or two ago – in North America as in many parts of Europe – was to maintain a smooth-running organisation and harmonious staff relationships. Schools functioned in the belief that teachers were competent and needed to be left alone to teach. As Leithwood and Montgomery (1982) have shown in Canadian elementary schools, principals of the 1980s did not see it as their role to attempt to improve their schools' 'instructional effectiveness'. That was not the job they had set themselves, nor was it the one they were expected to do.

Expectations of headteachers have changed, or are changing, in many national and state contexts and the very notion of leadership is closely bound in with their culture and history. Some school systems give greater weight to it than others but for the four countries of our study, education reforms have brought issues of school effectiveness sharply into the foreground and along with it the accountability of principals for school performance. Denmark has perhaps felt this wind of change most. Denmark has always been a school system which believed in a bottom-up approach, priding itself on its democracy and its strong focus on teacher autonomy. In recent years, however, school leaders have acquired greater responsibilities for developing the professional competence of staff, at the same time holding on to their primary task of allowing freedom for the individual classroom teacher to develop his or her relationship with pupils and with their parents. This focus on the individual teacher is not unique to Danish schools. France and Switzerland, for example, have historically shared that perspective. This exchange in 1996 between an English member of the research team and a Swiss researcher illustrates some of the assumptions which are effortlessly brought to the discussion of issues:

> English researcher to Swiss colleague:
> I'm very interested in the role of headteachers or school principals – who they are, and how they go about their job. Tell me, what are their main responsibilities in Switzerland?
> (pause)
> Swiss researcher (somewhat puzzled):
> Well, they make sure that the mail is given out.

In Swiss primary schools, there is commonly no head teacher, only a lead teacher who takes on minor administrative duties. The idea of a school with only teachers and no superordinate authority is deeply challenging to British heads and provokes a flood of questions. While answers to such questions might suggest the need to flatten the hierarchy of British schools, the context of international exchange and policy-borrowing is in fact pushing the Swiss and the French more towards a management model.

School principals in Queensland, like their counterparts in other parts of Australia (most notably Victoria), are being drawn increasingly into an accountability framework which will require them to take stronger professional leadership within their schools. In both Scotland and England, the power of the headteacher has been reinforced by increasing pay differentials between them and other staff. Headteachers in both countries are expected to be leading professionals within the school but this responsibility has to be balanced against major financial responsibilities and management demands. England, which has gone furthest down the road of self-government of the four countries in the study, places the most stringent governance and accountability framework on its headteachers.

The context and emphasis of school leadership may vary but increasingly it is the individual – the headteacher or school principal – who is placed in the spotlight. In England, for example, few of the headteachers of the 340 schools which had been designated as 'requiring special measures' following an Ofsted inspection, have remained in post after a critical inspection report (Riley and Rowles, 1996). But with all this focus on the individual, do we know what an 'effective' headteacher looks like? And is an 'effective' headteacher also a 'good' headteacher? How do those questions relate to the debates about what constitutes a 'good' school, as opposed to what constitutes an 'effective' school?

THE 'GOOD' SCHOOL AND THE 'EFFECTIVE' SCHOOL

The notion of what constitutes a good school is bound up in history, culture and local context.

> Good schools have been ones which have trained girls to be good wives and mothers, or which trained boys to serve the commercial ethic or the Empire. 'Good' has been an infinitely adaptable epithet, used of schools, of many kinds, by interested parties of many kinds.
>
> (Silver, 1994, p. 6)

The terms of 'good' and 'effective' are not neutral but contested. The notion of a good school is a social construct, shaped by national expectations and local aspirations. Equally, the notion of an effective school is socially constructed. Both notions rest on a belief that schools can make a difference but what those differences are may be at issue.

The basic assertion of the research literature on school effectiveness is that individual schools can make a difference to student achievement. Most of the early research on school effectiveness challenged the findings of James Coleman's highly influential US report on schools (Coleman et al., 1966) which had reached the conclusion that differences between one school and another only accounted for a small percentage of the variance in pupil performance. Subsequent studies (Brimer et al., 1978; Rutter et al., 1979) concluded that there were differences in the 'effectiveness' of schools greater than those identified in the Coleman study. These findings were endorsed by a further study (Mortimore et al., 1988) which examined primary schools in London and identified a range of variables (including leadership style) which could have positive effects on student outcomes.

The studies provided a welcome challenge to the social pathology of failure. They began to paint details into the portrait of what an effective school or classroom should look like (Silver, 1994, p. 93). Critics have argued, however, that research findings have become used as blanket recipes – solutions to the problems facing all schools. Research findings on school effectiveness were treated as 'laws of science that applied to all schools and all teachers' (Glickman, 1987, quoted in Silver 1994, p. 102); Purkey and Smith (1983), in one of the first such critiques, concluded that school effectiveness research tended to ignore school culture and issues of organisational change, and concluded that the characteristics which school effectiveness emphasised were

unlikely to work in all schools, may not work as expected in many schools, and may in fact be counterproductive in some schools.
    (Purkey and Smith, 1983, pp. 440 and 447, quoted in Silver, 1994, p. 98)

More recently, critics have charged the movement with ignoring the social and economic content (Stoll and Riley, 1997, Whitty, 1997). Others have criticised it for being platitudinous, re-inventing the obvious; missing the fine-grain reality of school life; appropriating language (e.g. 'effectiveness'); misdirecting attention from wider structural issues; confusing correlations and causes; offering little to school management or teachers; ignoring the problematic of the curriculum; and limited in its focus on the school as an entity (White and Barber, 1997).

By the very nature of its construction, school effectiveness research is vulnerable to such attacks. Its findings often seem no more than commonsensical. Its concern for quantifiable, reliable measures does limit its compass. Its focus on the internal workings of the school does, by definition, exclude home, community and wider political contexts. Silver (1994) has argued that schools operate within three sets of realities:

- the community location (the social needs and neighbourhood context);
- the policy context (set at the national and state level); and
- the internal workings (how the school perceives and acts upon its responsibilities).

Evidence from an English study of schools which have 'failed' Ofsted inspections (Riley and Rowles, 1996) suggests that a combination of pressures pushes schools along the downward spiral. Some of those pressures relate to weak leadership and isolated and disaffected staff (that is, the internal working of the school) but the study also demonstrated that many such schools served areas of deprivation and high unemployment (that is, the community location) and most of the secondary schools were in competition with selective grammar schools, or grant-maintained schools (that is, the policy context).

School effectiveness does, deliberately and specifically, focus on schools and has been unapologetically directed at explaining what goes on within the black box. Its strength and unique contribution to our understanding of schools is also its most singular weakness, however. The need to control the variables such as home background requires that these things are factored out, so risking the loss of data on the most significant area for enhancement of learning, the dynamic relationship between what pupils bring to school and what they take away from school (MacBeath, 1998).

The focus on individual schools is also a limiting factor. As Benn and Chitty (1996) have pointed out, the efforts of any individual school are affected by the organisation of other schools in the neighbourhood. The contextual effect, the critical mass, or the critical mix, is not just an intra-school phenomenon but an inter-school one. Effective schools are not just a product of the social dynamics within their four walls but a result of the wider social dynamic of the neighbourhood and the larger political and economic processes at work.

Attainment measures, however much used as proxies and surrounded by health warnings, may, nonetheless, reinforce a deeply-entrenched view of effective schools as those most efficient at improving exam scores. Where this happens, researchers may be wittingly or unwittingly complicit in diverting attention from wider structural issues and political agendas or fail to challenge retrogressive views of what education is or what schools might be for. In a critique of Rutter's (1979) work, Holtz, for example, argued that

> As we acknowledge the important contribution of 'Fifteen Thousand Hours' and other . . . research of its kind, it may be worth our while to remember that we once hoped that schools would create new models of community, encourage new commitments towards meaningful vocations, end racial discrimination, and open up new avenues out of poverty and unhappiness. Right now, it seems we rejoice if children can be taught to read.
>
> (Holtz, 1981, quoted in Silver, 1994, p. 102)

A similar view has been expressed by Gammage who argued that school effectiveness research, and its policy emphasis, obscured thinking about the 'good' school. This he characterised as one which focused on relationships, the nature of the school community, its essential values, and its capacity to enrich the lives of those who are a part of it:

> Perhaps therefore the good school is that which most successfully matches its curricular organisation and ethos to an expectation of high commitment by children . . . a school is 'good' not such much because of the specific nature of what is taught (though that is important) but through the manner in which a positive, supportive, richly and frequently interactive atmosphere is created.
>
> (Gammage, 1985, quoted in Silver 1994, p. 101)

The effective school is only one version of a good school and only one contributor to our understanding of what good schools are and how they come into being. Without a constant reminder of this, the danger is that broader notions of schooling and good schools drop off the policy and improvement agenda. In a recent paper on school effectiveness for the British Psychological Society, Raven (1997) made the case for deriving criteria of effectiveness from perceptions of the goals of education held by pupils, parents, teachers and employers. He argued that these give us better measures for differentiating 'more' from 'less' effective performance in occupational and life roles.

In fact there has been a growing rapprochement of school effectiveness and school improvement. A study for the National Union of Teachers (MacBeath et al., 1995) which did derive effectiveness criteria from the stakeholders mentioned by Raven, found a close match between what parents, pupils and teachers wanted from their schools and what the mainstream of effectiveness research had identified. The school 'insiders' did, however, bring to those criteria, a depth of insight and elaboration of what learning and good schools meant. Good schools were those whose culture provided opportunities for growth, not only for pupils but for teachers and school leaders. The importance of such a culture is expressed by Per Dalin, the Norwegian educator, in these terms:

> The only way schools will survive the future is to become creative learning organisations. The best way students can learn how to live in the future is to experience the life of the learning school.
>
> (Dalin with Rolff, 1995, p. 19)

The work of Dalin and other school improvers in fact owes much to the effectiveness movement. It is a broadening church. It is more welcoming of practitioners and more willing to test its findings in school and classroom practice. The growing percentage of teachers and headteachers who attend and present papers at the annual School Effectiveness/School Improvement conferences is a vital sign of a learning movement which welcomes challenge and seeks a closer inter-relationship between theory and practice.

These are important issues to be borne in mind when considering the relationship between effective leadership and effective schools. They are in part about terminology but in larger part about values and paradigms, ways of thinking and ways of seeing.

EFFECTIVENESS OF LEADERSHIP

Our use of the term 'effective' in terms of leadership is not derived from any empirical correlation with student attainment nor indeed from any outcome measures of school performance. Effectiveness, we recognise, is a contested notion and one that has to remain open to question, to challenge and to refinement. Deriving definitions of 'effectiveness' in leadership from the views of stakeholders, proved to be a useful starting place and the following 'expert' view from a group of nine year-olds in our project lays a useful groundwork. They described a good headteacher in these terms:

- Has a good education and is able to solve problems
- Is very experienced as a teacher
- Is able to understand children – what they can do at different ages
- Is easy going but firm
- Knows how to look after the building and create a nice environment and a safe place for children
- Knows how to take responsibility for things happening in the school and does not blame others
- Is able to make children, adults and the community feel confident about the things they do in school
- Provides a good example in their behaviour (by not smoking, or drinking in school)
- Is not racist and makes others see that the colour of their skin does not matter
- Keeps in touch with the local community, letting them know what is happening in the school
- Treats children equally
- Gives everyone the same advantages.

(Quoted in Riley, 1998a, p. 122)

The view of leadership offered by this group of children proved to be a consistent theme within our study. Effective leadership meant sustaining those relationships within a community in which all its members are heard, and taken account of. A happy and fulfilling school experience may stay with children right into their adult life and make it more likely that they would return to formal education as adults at a later stage. Paying attention to the inner life of the school was described as a requisite of leadership over a hundred years ago:

> The organisation of the school must be kept mobile to its inner life. To one who is accustomed to wind up the machine and trust it to run for fixed periods, this constantly shifting shape of things will seem unsafe and troublesome. And troublesome it is; for no fixed plan can be followed; no two schools are alike; and the same school is shifting, requiring constant attention and nimble judgement on the part of the (school leader).
>
> (Arnold Tomkins, education pioneer New York State, 1895, quoted in Louis et al., 1995)

The school leadership paradigm which emerges from our study emphasises the capability of the school leader to sustain relationships. It is a model which ties in closely with much of the thinking about school improvement (e.g. Stoll and Fink, 1992) and which puts the heart and emotions of teaching at the centre (Hargreaves, 1997). The paradigm is also one of mobility and fragility. It rests on the assumption (inherent in Arnold Tomkins's analysis) that schools are constantly changing. The challenge is to be able to respond to the school's inner life – troublesome though it may be – as well to the demanding and constantly changing external context. It recognises that schools have to serve internal and external constituencies which are often in uneasy relationship with one another. It acknowledges that school leaders have to manage contested notions about achievement and cope with multiple interests and demands. It rests on uncertainty, as well as certainty, and is rooted in a deep understanding of context – national, local and school-based. It is because of this complexity that no single recipe will work.

The school leadership paradigm is also one of shared leadership. School leadership is beyond the undertakings of one heroic individual. It is simply not possible, and may not even be desirable, for one individual to undertake every leadership task within a school. Good school leaders are those who are able to maximise the diverse leadership qualities of others, enabling them to take on leadership within their areas of expertise. They lead by managing, motivating and inspiring people. This may come through individual one-to-one work with teachers, pupils, parents or governors, or through creating the impetus within an organisation that encourages and enables people to play an active part in school life. They are clear about 'the vision business' and recognise that whilst national targets and performance criteria have to be satisfied, those external goals can only be achieved by creating a professional community within the school. As one headteacher in our study concluded:

> My job is to try and develop the collegiate nature of the school and to create the opportunities for staff to develop professional relationships with colleagues in other schools.
>
> (Quoted in Riley, 1998b).

Good leaders who operate in this way recognise that teachers are more likely to become engaged in making changes within their own schools when more collaborative leadership models are the norm. As Gammage (1985) implied in his account of the good school, good leaders recognise the importance of relationships, enrichment and an interactive community. The style is also an inclusive one, for the reasons suggested by the findings from this North American study:

> Teachers' willingness to participate in school decision-making is influenced primarily by their relationships with their principals. . . . Teachers appear more willing to participate in all areas of decision-making if they perceive their relationships with their principals as more open, collaborative, facilitative and supportive. They are less willing to participate in any decision-making if they characterize their relationships with the principals as closed, exclusionary, and controlling.
>
> (Smylie, 1992, p. 63 quoted in Murphy, 1994, p. 30)

The other key element in our paradigm is that school leadership is about making choices, deciding on priorities, and being willing to learn and change. The model cannot be transposed from one situation, or context, to another because it is not a static model. It relies on the ability of the leaders to revise his or her approach and to learn and reflect. The capacity to be a continual learner is key. A Canadian review of school leaders con-cluded that 'effective' leaders were good role models in their school who set an example by 'working hard, having lots of energy, being genuine in their beliefs, modelling openness, having good people skills, and by showing evidence of learning by growing and changing themselves' (Leithwood et al., 1997). Priorities and emphasis may change but values will remain constant.

School leaders have to make choices not only about what they do but about how they do it. The people with whom headteachers spend their time give telling insights into values, priorities, contexts and the underlying rationale for those choices. Danish headteachers in our study spent much more of their working day with teachers than Scottish or English heads. Scottish headteachers spent considerably more time with pupils than their Danish and English counterparts, while English heads were more likely to spend their time with outside agencies or individuals, managing external politics.

The people headteachers spend their time with does not, of course, indicate how they spend it. A headteacher who spends time with staff may be doing qualitatively different things, for example, nurturing, supporting, developing, or being task-orientated about specific elements of the school day (for example, the time-table). Time spent with pupils could imply disciplinary matters (poor performance); or personal issues (such as home pressures); or appreciation of educational achievements. Our analysis suggests that good headteachers are able to recognise how they spend their time, with whom and for what purposes, and then link their behaviour to their priorities. There are choices to be made and these choices may change, depending on the circumstances of the school, as well as the local and national environments. Effective leadership is about making those choices and about managing the 'fit' between the external world and the internal world of the school.

Analysis of the comparative data within and between the countries in our study suggests that there are a number of key dimensions which distinguish different approaches to leadership on the part of the headteacher. We have identified three that recur quite consistently. These are not all of the dimensions, nor are they necessarily definitive, but they do illustrate the complexities of leadership and its active and interactive nature. These three dimensions can be represented as three intersecting axes on which any given headteacher could be placed, or might place him/herself.

The internal-external dimension distinguishes between headteachers who look primarily inwards to the school community and those who look outwards to the local, or wider community. Philosophically, this might be distinguished by overt beliefs such as 'I believe I must protect and market

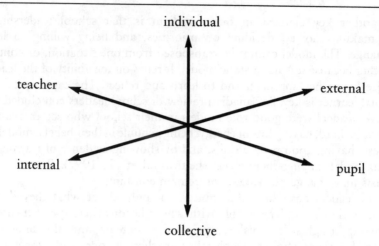

the school', as against 'my job is to be with children and teachers'. Or it might spring less from conviction than circumstance and context.

The individual-collective dimension distinguishes between philosophy and behaviour which is orientated towards individual pupils and members of staff as against the broader collective. Some headteachers used staff meetings and collective occasions, such as school assemblies, to foster a corporate identity. Some used self-evaluation, staff development and forward planning as collective mechanisms to demonstrate that decision-making was a corporate enterprise. At the other end of the spectrum, a headteacher might prefer a more individualistic style of influence, working through key individuals, using sanctions and rewards to promote (or marginalise) key players. Some school leaders spent time with individual pupils and with individual members of staff, encouraging, motivating, counselling, sanctioning and disciplining, and in some cases grooming individuals for promotion. As with the first dimension, these are tendencies, rather than diametrically-opposite patterns of behaviour, and the dimension could oversimplify what may be a complex and even inconsistent mix. Again, behaviour on this dimension is a matter of both national and local culture, as well as deriving from school-based factors.

The pupil-centred/teacher-centred dimension is even more difficult to see as ends of one continuous axis. However, we have tried to distinguish what has emerged clearly from the data – time priority given to being with pupils, or being with teachers. Some headteachers spent a great deal of the day with pupils, in either a teaching or counselling/disciplinary situation. Others saw little of pupils and spent more time with teachers, individually or collectively. This could reflect a difference in philosophy between those who saw pupils as the focus for development and those who saw teachers as the vehicle for change. Other school leaders put greater emphasis on time with staff and on staff needs. Their implicit or overt philosophy was that pupils would be the ultimate beneficiaries of an attempt to meet the needs of staff.

These three dimensions are complex, shifting, dynamically inter-related and real. They differ by country (which can be related to cultural and historic factors) and by school sector. Primary heads are more likely to spend time with pupils in a teaching-learning situation and with teachers on curriculum development than secondary heads. They report less lobbying and fewer tensions among group interests than their secondary colleagues (who have to contend with vertical department divisions, and layers of hierarchical responsibility).

Differences are also capricious and determined by happenstance, as well as by individual style. School leaders operate in particular ways because that is what they have always done, or what people have done before them. Sometimes they choose to act in new ways as a reaction to the past. We concluded that school leaders need to be aware of 'who' they are spending their time with, as well as the 'why' and the 'how'. The allocation of time reflects implicit priorities. Effective headteachers can match the two in ways that relate to their context, their own skills and attributes, as well as changing circumstances.

CONCLUDING THOUGHTS

The exploration of school leadership presented in this chapter suggests that there are a number of tensions in thinking about models of leadership. Leadership is bound in context but whilst it does not lend itself to recipe swapping, discussions about common ingredients can be helpful. The conceptualisation of school leadership presented here acknowledges instability, the quixotic natures of schools and their political and social location, unlike some of the school effectiveness literature which has tended to deal in categoricals, and to focus on quantifiable outcomes and measurements of performance. 'Effective' school leaders are also 'good' leaders. They are distinguished by their vision and passion and by their capacity to bring a critical spirit into the complex and demanding job of headship, whilst at the same time focusing on staff and pupil performance, and on classroom pedagogy.

REFERENCES

Benn, C. and Chitty, C. (1996) *Thirty Years On: Is Comprehensive Education Alive and Well or Struggling to Survive?*, David Fulton, London.

Brimer, A. et al. (1978) *Sources of Difference in School Achievement*, National Foundation for Educational Research, Slough.

Coleman, J. S. et al. (1966) *Equality of Educational Opportunity*, Department of Health, Education and Welfare, Washington DC.

Dalin, P. with Rolff, H. G. (1995) *Changing the School Culture*, Cassell, London.

Gammage, P. (1985) *What is a Good School?*, National Association for Primary Education, University of Nottingham.

Glickman, C. D. (1987) Good and/or effective schools: what do we want?, *Phi Delta Kappan*, Vol. 68, no. 8, pp. 622–624.

Hargreaves, A. (1997) Feeling like a teacher: The emotions of teaching and educational, change. Paper submitted to *Phi Delta Kappan*.

Holtz, B. W. (1981) Can schools make a differences? (review of Rutter et al., *Fifteen Thousand Hours*), *Teachers College Record*, Vol. 83, no. 2, pp. 300–7.

Leithwood, K. and Montgomery, D (1982) The role of the elementary principal in program improvement *Review of Educational Research*, Vol. 52 no. 3, pp. 309–339.

Leithwood, K., Leonard, L. and Sharratt, S. (1997) Conditions fostering organisational learning in schools. Paper given at the International Congress for School Effectiveness and Improvement, Memphis, USA, 5–8 January.

Louis, K. S., Kruse, S. and Associates (1995) *Professionalism and Community: Perspectives on Reforming Urban Schools*, Corwin Press, Thousand Oaks, California.

MacBeath, J., Boyd, B., Rand, J. and Bell, S. (1995) *Schools Speak for Themselves*, National Union of Teachers, London.

MacBeath, J., Moos, L. and Riley, K. A. (1996) Leadership in a changing world, in K. Leithwood, K. Chapman, C. Corson, P. Hallinger, P. and A. Hart (eds.) *International Handbook for Educational Leadership and Administration*, Kluwer, Dordrecht.

Mortimore, P., Sammons, P., Stoll, L., Lewis, D. and Ecob, R. (1988) *School Matters: The Junior School Years*, Open Books, London.

Murphy, J. (1994) Transformational change and the evolving role of the principal, in J. Murphy and K. Seashore Louis (eds.) *Reshaping the Principalship: Insights from Transformational Reform Efforts*, Corwin Press, Thousand Oaks, California.

Purkey, S. C. and Smith, M. D. (1983) Effective Schools: a review, *The Elementary School Journal*, Vol. 83, no. 1, p. 429.

Raven, J. (1997) Education, educational research, ethics and the BPS, in *British Pyschological Society Education Section Review*, Vol. No. 21 pp. 3–10

Riley, K. A. (1998a) *Whose School is it Anyway?* Falmer Press, London.

Riley, K. A. (1998b) Creating the Leadership Climate, *International Journal of Leadership in Education*, Vol 1, no. 2.

Riley, K. A. and Rowles, D. (1996) *Learning from Failure*, London Borough of Haringey.

Rutter, M., Maughan, B., Mortimore, P., Ouston, J. with Smith, A. (1979) *Fifteen Thousand Hours: Secondary Schools and their Effects on Children*, Open Books, London.

Sammons, P., Hillman, J. and Mortimore, P. (1995) *Key Characteristics of Effective Schools: A Review of School Effectiveness*, Research for the Office of Standards in Education, London.

Silver, H. (1994) *Good Schools, Effective Schools*, Cassell, London.

Smylie, M. A. (1992) Teacher participation in school decision making: assessing willingness to participate, *Educational Evaluation and Policy Analysis*, Vol. 14, no. 1, pp. 53–67.

Stoll, L. and Fink, D. (1992) Effecting school change: the Halton approach, *School Effectiveness and School Improvement*, Vol. 3, no. 1, pp. 19–41.

Stoll, L. and Riley, K. A. (1998) School effectiveness and school improvement, *Country Report to the International Conference on School Effectiveness and Improvement*, Manchester, January.

White, J. and Barber, M. (eds.) (1997) *Perspectives on School Effectiveness and School Improvement*, Institute of Education, London.

Whitty, G. (1997) Social Theory and Education. Social Policy: the Karl Mannheim Memorial Lecture, London Institute of Education.

10

Developing Effective School Leaders

Jenny Reeves and Neil Dempster

INTRODUCTION

In this chapter, we concentrate on several aspects of our work related to the professional development of headteachers. In the introduction to the book we described the methods we used in England, Scotland, Denmark which were planned as a collaborative activity involving principals and researchers and contributing to an unfolding research design. We found this particularly helpful because as data were gathered and processed they were analysed and discussed by all parties before planning for the next stage. In this way, all participants whether headteachers or researchers could set their own knowledge and experience in a wider context and fuller information base. This gave us new perspectives for interpreting and understanding the findings and framing new questions.

At the heart of this approach was a concern to understand better the expectations of school leaders and what was being asked of them by governors, parents, teachers, pupils and members of the community.

Three elements of the study have a particular relevance for the professional development of school leaders. Firstly there is the research process itself as a vehicle for critical reflection. Secondly, a number of instruments were developed during the process which could be adapted for use by other groups. Thirdly, some of the findings have a direct bearing on support for professional development and school improvement.

COLLABORATIVE RESEARCH MODELS

Using a collaborative research process as a vehicle for professional development is probably best suited to projects with a fairly large group of school leaders. There are benefits for practitioners in collaborating with professional researchers in the collection and processing of data but this does mean that the focus of enquiry must stand in its own right as a research exercise. Additionally, a larger group, particularly a cross-cultural one, allows for a richness of data and variety of approaches to analysis and can therefore open up a range of issues which might be less easily identified in a small group.

The advantages of using a collaborative model of research for professional development are:

- it helps to ensure that the research is related to practice and subject to scrutiny for professional relevance as it proceeds;
- since it requires constant re-examination of practice it is fundamentally a learning process for those involved;
- there is some in-built cognitive dissonance in that practitioners and researchers bring different perspectives to the research questions and to the interpretation of the data. This requires members of both groups to question certain of their assumptions;
- it allows for the efficient use of resources so that the practitioners can engage in what is illuminating and interesting to them rather than wrestling with data gathering and processing skills which are not really relevant to their job. At the same time, the disciplines of the research process try to ensure the most appropriate and rigorous structure.

The power of the research is enhanced by virtue of the fact that it draws on people from different cultural backgrounds, magnifying its educative power while at the same time creating its own difficulties and complexities.

Two aspects of the collaborative research process are of particular interest to us:

- How the individual cases and general findings relate to one another and can help people to begin to see themselves and their practice as part of a wider context
- How a generic model for use by other groups might be derived from the project.

RELATING PERSONAL EXPERIENCE TO A WIDER CONTEXT

One of the most interesting features of the Effective Leadership in a Time of Change project was that, whilst working from a data base which centred on individual school leaders and their experiences, we were able to show links between their personal perceptions and many of the current themes in school leadership and management including major policy shifts of the late 1980s and 1990s. There has often been a tendency in designing professional development to rely on the presentation of theoretical and generic issues and then to leave it to participants to relate this to their own situation. Certainly our experience demonstrates the potential of proceeding the other way about.

Having data from a fairly large number of respondents, and the potential to subject it to analyses of different kinds, opened up different ways of examining the role of school leaders. With information on gender, age, time in post, school size, school type and nationality for each respondent we were able to look for patterns and emphases among the many qualities which they had identified as important in being an effective head.

For instance, the emphases on certain qualities of headteachers highlighted quite marked differences according to the nationality of the respondent. This opened up debate within the group about how far management style was a product of national/cultural forces, leading back into a deeper questioning of certain current orthodoxies. How far could the findings on effective school leadership and management in one cultural context legitimately be applied across national borders as many politicians appeared to be trying to do? It also allowed individuals to begin to raise questions such as 'why is it that we (as headteachers) in Scotland do x in a particular way? Should we be developing a different approach?'

Some variations in national responses appeared to relate to deep-seated cultural differences whilst others seemed to be better explained by the differing political agendas in the countries concerned. This was of particular interest to participating heads because it could be seen that a common reform agenda was being played out in slightly different ways in each of the participating countries. This raised issues such as the desirability of the Danes learning from the experiences of their English colleagues. Might this help them to avoid some of the consequences of the way in which issues of accountability had been handled there?

In the same way analysis by gender raised questions about differences between the approaches of men and women headteachers. Were there consistent differences in role and performance of the role? If there were such differences, were they simply a product of the headteacher's own personal style or did the stereotypes held by staff, pupils and parents limit the range of behaviours and strategies which a head might adopt? Comparison of the more biographical details contained in the interviews revealed other gender differences. For instance, the ways in which women came into the job differed significantly from that of their male colleagues. This raised issues about the nature of the professional support that heads should be offering to their more junior colleagues.

These forms of feedback were particularly powerful in engaging project team members in examining their own roles because they knew that the outcomes of the various analyses arose directly from their own feedback to the research team. They had a personal investment in seeking to interpret and understand the outcomes.

We have tried to illustrate this relationship between the personal and the general in Figure 10.1 to show how the various categories for analysis provided the link to a wider context for interpretation. This was not a one-way process because it also allowed project members to make links in the opposite direction from the general back to their own specific situation.

The focus on expectations and personal professional biography, particularly within a group drawn from different national contexts, helped both headteachers and researchers to challenge previously unexamined assumptions and some of the 'givens' of their own particular cultural context. The use of research techniques to collect, analyse and feed back the data gave

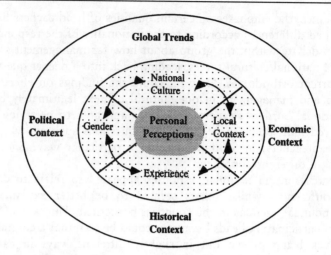

Figure 10.1   Relating the personal to a wider context

group members a powerful basis for adopting a critical perspective on their own development and making their experience meaningful within a political, historical and cultural framework (Apple, 1993).

GENERALISING THE RESEARCH PROCESS

In generalising the research process we used, we are conscious that there is no one recipe for the conduct of investigations into school leadership and management issues. However, in order to use research to support professional development we suggest a sequence of ten steps. We suggest that there are generic qualities which can be applied in different and changing contexts. The steps are written as guidelines for headteachers working in partnerships with colleagues.

Step 1

Identify a persistent problem that is troubling you as a school leader. Check your impressions of the problem with other heads and debate whether it is sufficiently significant to warrant systematic investigation.

Step 2

If it is agreed that the issue is broadly troublesome, form a research task group of interested colleagues and a researcher or two and together define the overarching research problem. This is a very important part in the process so a few pointers about research problems may help.

A research problem is usually composed from what, how, who, where and when questions but should always include a why. Three different examples are provided below to help newly-formed task groups get started.

- What are the expectations of school leaders? How do they affect school leadership and why and by whom are they held?
- What happens during staff appraisal and why does it happen in the way that it does?
- Who is affected when the league tables are published? Are the effects felt differently by parents, teachers and students and if so, why?

Spending plenty of time on getting the research problem clear will pay off in the long run as all members of the task group come to share a common understanding of the matters that need to be investigated.

Step 3

The third step involves the task group discussing and deciding what purposes the research should serve. Research purposes and problems are directly linked. The overarching research problem helps us to focus on what data we need about the phenomenon under investigation so that we can achieve our purposes. The research purposes indicate how we want to use the data. For most school-focused research, two purposes are critical:

(i) to develop an understanding of the problem being investigated; and
(ii) to utilise that understanding to reflect on current practice in order to improve it.

Step 4

In the fourth step, the members of the task group flesh out the research problem into a set of general and specific questions. An example from the Australian study is reproduced to show how these kinds of questions were derived from our overarching research problem, which was:

What are the expectations of school leaders?, How do they affect school leadership and why and by whom are they held?

In the example below the general question is followed by selected specific questions:

What are the expectations of school principals held by different stakeholders?

(a) What do you feel that parents and staff expect of you in your leadership of the school?
(b) What pressures do you experience from government, state and regional officers?

(c) What is your perception of what students expect of their principal?

(d) What does the wider community want of you as school leader?

The list of general and specific questions does not have to be long. In fact, you may restrict yourselves to the development of general questions only at this stage. Whichever approach you take, disciplined attention must be given to generating these questions by the task group. They are essential if the research process is to lead to productive professional development.

Step 5

In Step 5, data gathering begins with you and members of the task group providing responses to the general and specific questions you have developed. You can do this in a number of ways:

1. Task group members can prepare individual, written responses to each general question and its specific questions on a prepared recording sheet.

2. Responses can be recorded by using a group procedure. A chairperson puts each question to the group and members record their responses on slips of paper, one response only to each slip of paper.

3. Case study interviews using the set of general and specific questions can be carried out with each member of the task group.

4. Journals can be kept by each task group member for a nominated period, enabling responses to be written at a more leisurely pace.

It has often been said that our decisions are only as good as our information and so gathering the views of task group members provides each individual immediately with a wider perspective on the research problem. It also asks all involved to suspend judgement until adequate data have been processed.

Step 6

Now initial data processing is undertaken usually covering the two steps:

1. Coding. This involves nominating the categories into which responses will be arranged.

2. Collating. Once the codes have been agreed, like responses are collated under each code heading, with a record being produced as a table or matrix or a set of summary statements.

The last step, analysing and interpreting, should be carried out by the task group as a whole. Here, concentration is on what the summary statements are telling you, singly or taken together, what the main themes in the responses are and why you have obtained the results you have.

Step 7

Follow-up data gathering is now planned, prepared and conducted by the task group. This is the process through which the general and specific questions are pursued with other people whose views have a direct bearing on the overarching research question. This is a critical step in making the research process a professional development strategy because it treats the knowledge gained from the analysis and interpretation of task group perceptions as tentative. It acknowledges the need for confirmation or disconfirmation before actions about the problem are taken. If you use this approach you can construct a questionnaire for other groups in the following way:

(a) head sheets of paper with the codes or categories against which you collated your own responses;
(b) under each heading list key words or phrases used as responses to the general and specific questions;
(c) turn these words or phrases into items for the questionnaire.

The example taken from our study below shows one of the codes or categories produced from our interviews and the items we developed from the words and phrases of our participating principals.

The Code or Category: Expectations related to the management of change
The Items:

I expect the principal: SA A D SD
(Strongly Agree, Agree,
Disagree, Strongly Disagree)

1. to change dominant values in the school community
2. to protect the school from unrealistic external demands
3. to prioritise issues of change
4. to keep change to a minimum
5. to spend money on changing the school

Questionnaire design is difficult but, as you can see, it is easier when you are using raw material you already have at your disposal. Your task group may need to look for help on good questionnaire design if it does not contain a member with that expertise. Of course you do not have to use a questionnaire in follow-up data gathering. What we emphasise, however, is that initial data gathering should be complemented by follow-up data gathering to ensure the credibility of the findings.

Step 8

Step 8 involves the task group in bringing initial and follow-up data together. Here there is a need to compare and contrast results from different respondents so that similarities and differences are noted. The dominant view of one group of respondents may not be that of another. Getting to know the data well for each group and being able to identify where ideas coincide is an important outcome of this step in the process.

Step 9

This penultimate step is designed to distil major messages from the analysis of the data. Members are asked to address two synthesising questions. The first is answered as individuals – 'What have I learned from our work?' Members discuss their personal responses before turning to the second question – 'What have we learned about the overarching research problem?'. This is addressed as a group.

Step 10

The final step in the process concentrates on translating personal and collective learning into action, beginning with the question: If this is what we have learned, what do we want to do about it? The answers to this question will result in identifying the aims and objectives you and others wish to achieve to improve the situation in your school.

Our intention here is to show how the research design and its methods can provide a particularly useful professional development strategy which may be applied to other important areas of school leadership. There are many issues confronting today's school leaders which merit study – How effective are strategic planning and review processes? Where do the difficulties lie in ethical decision-making? Why is power sharing with parent and community members so troublesome? How strongly is curriculum development influenced by market forces? Is there a balance possible in the headteacher's advisory and appraisal roles? How can leadership and management competence be judged? These are but a few of the issues on which the learning of heads might be focused.

SOME TOOLS AND TECHNIQUES TO AID CRITICAL REFLECTION

For smaller, relatively homogenous groups, some of the instruments and techniques we developed can be easily adapted to help people reflect continually on their own practice without necessarily being part of a formal research project.

1   Images of leadership – tapping into personal professional issues

One way of looking at school leadership is for headteachers (and others) to tap into their own feelings and perceptions without having to use a verbal form of communication. The exercise we used at the start of the project, in which we asked people to draw what it felt like to be a school leader, provided unexpected and often deep insights into roles and contexts of leadership. The drawings served to open up discussion and tap into a number of shared issues for the group relatively quickly.

2 Looking at the relationship between beliefs and behaviour

This is a crucial process in developing the basis for critical reflection on practice and improving professional expertise (Tripp, 1993). In our case, this arose from our desire to explore the extent to which expectations of effective leadership were in tension with routine administrative tasks.

This was tackled by asking heads to identify their own expectations of effective headship and then to keep a detailed log of how they spent their time.

This same model can be used to identify expectations of the good headteacher using:

- either a standard list of qualities, attributes and behaviours to select from such as that we derived from our own study or a similar list drawn from other studies
- or deriving their own lists from responses to the question 'What do you think makes for a good headteacher?'

If you are working in a cross-national group, it is better to derive the list from direct questions rather than use a pre-selected list which may not be applicable to members of the group because it fails to reflect their culture.

People might also be asked to keep a diary on a small sample of days (two or three) providing detailed information about their own day-to-day practice using categories such as the following:

Time usage	Length of time and type of task (at fifteen minute intervals)
Contacts	Staff/Children/Parents/Other
Content	For instance, if you talked to a teacher, was it about an administrative, curricular or a personal matter?
Location	Office, classroom, staffroom, playground out of school.
Feelings	How you felt about the task/interaction at the time.

By comparing the two – a school leader's view of what is important in leadership with what he or she does on a day-to-day basis – you can begin to address the question of how far people meet their own expectations of their role. By sharing and comparing individual results, the group can also open up the whole issue of leadership style and how this relates to effectiveness.

Within a fairly large mixed group you can also use these two data sources in combination with some basic information about group members (gender, nationality, time in post, school type or size etc.) to look at similarities and differences in the approach to school leadership examining dimensions such as gender, type of school and cultural background.

3   Examining situational and developmental issues

Another tool for examining practice is to use evidence about a school leader's career in post in a more structured way. Group members draw up their own career path on a timeline showing high and low points along it. The timeline should run from the point at which he or she was appointed as a school leader to the present time. Important periods/events within their headship are then highlighted and people write short descriptions of these, recording the nature of their feelings and thoughts at the time.

These timelines can then be used by the group as a basis for comparing and contrasting experiences and coming to a better understanding of career patterns. It opens up debate about why differences in behaviour occur at different stages and the reasons for these changes. It also raises issues about the variation in school contexts and how the situation influences leadership style. It helps group members to see their experience in a wider perspective and to think about how they might respond to their own stage of development in context more effectively.

4   Taking account of the expectations of others

The project also developed survey instruments for use with students, teachers, parents and school board members to help them explore the expectations of a good school leader from differing points of view.

Where such a survey is impractical, another approach is to work with focus groups using a card-sort exercise based on a set of attributes for the good headteacher. This is probably a more practical exercise where a group does not have the capacity to analyse large amounts of data.

The outcomes from both surveys and card-sort exercises raised a number of interesting issues for the school leaders in our study and demonstrated the wide range of views they needed to take into account. It also showed where there were discrepancies between their own perceptions and those of their immediate constituencies.

SOME IMPLICATIONS OF THE FINDINGS FOR PROFESSIONAL DEVELOPMENT

One set of findings seemed particularly pertinent to the question of how best to support the professional development of headteachers. The outcomes of the research into the career patterns of school leaders both before and after their appointment raises a number of issues for those who have a role in planning and providing development opportunities for school leaders and managers (Chapter 3 and Reeves et al., 1997) .

Our investigation appeared to show a fairly consistent pattern of development in headship. In all, we identified eight stages in this process, each of which seemed to mark a qualitative change in the school leaders' experience and orientation to practice.

This 'career path' has far-reaching implications for fostering effective leadership. Enhanced effectiveness depends on patterns of support and professional development which are consonant with the way the individual develops and adjusts to the school context after his or her appointment.

It is clear that it would be helpful to new school leaders not simply to have been through management training (Dunning, 1996) but also to have been prepared for their own cycle of development including the emotional, intellectual and political demands of entry as a newly-appointed leader into an organisation which is new to them.

Joint training for management teams in schools would also seem to be a fruitful strategy for improving leadership effectiveness. An investment in team development at a relatively early stage after a new leader's appointment might well prove to be very cost effective in the long run given the number of accounts where the failure to develop a joint vision for the future of the school and good working relationships within the management team served to block development and consume people's energies.

An understanding of the developmental stages may well help more school leaders to develop the kind of relationship with their school which will foster real improvements in classroom practice. School leaders may well need help in recognising the kinds of changes they need to make in their own practice and to move from one stage to the next, unblocking impediments to change and progression. They may have become 'stuck' at the more superficial level of improvement because they lack either the understanding and/or the skills and self-confidence to move forward.

Equally, we need to address the issue of maintaining school leader's effectiveness and enthusiasm at later stages in their career and this in itself warrants further investigation into the reasons for the apparent decline which has been identified by numerous researchers (Weindling and Earley, 1998; Mortimore et al., 1988). Providing school leaders with the opportunity to reflect upon phases in career and the kinds of changes that the development cycle may require of them can help them make the appropriate responses in their own particular context.

The power of context (Leithwood et al., 1992) is a significant finding of our study. A lot of current training opportunities concentrate on generic topics which are largely de-contextualised but our study points to the need to pay much closer attention to the issues which arise for individuals in their particular situation and how these can be understood, confronted and resolved. This requires a greater emphasis on the development of professional problem-solving capabilities (Leithwood et al., 1992) in relation to school leadership. This is something which is often left to chance or informal peer mentoring rather than forming a central feature of professional development for school leaders.

BENEFITS OF PROFESSIONAL DEVELOPMENT THROUGH APPLIED RESEARCH

The processes we adopted bring together in modified form two well-recognised, professional development strategies, both with the potential to equip people with practical tools and powerful learning outcomes. The two strategies are 'action research' and 'narrative inquiry'. By action research, we refer to observing and reflecting on practice in order to learn from it so that future practice is improved. By narrative inquiry, we refer to the analysis of personal accounts of experience with a view to understanding and improving practice.

Authors such as Altricher et al. (1993) and Carr and Kemmis (1986) speak of the way in which action research helps people to learn from their experiences while scholars such as Connelly and Clandinin (1991) and Goodson and Walker (1991) talk about people making meaning from personal accounts in order to learn from them and from the accounts of others. Logan et al. (1996) put action and narrative inquiry together this way:

> Action research provides a process for identifying and clarifying a concern, setting and testing an hypothesis, collecting and analysing data. Narrative inquiry transforms the story of that process from a collective activity into a disciplined personal process confirming, disconfirming or creating professional practical knowledge.

> (1996, p. 79)

We suggest that the merging of action research and narrative inquiry produces a powerful professional development strategy which:

• uses a voluntarist, self-help approach to professional learning;
• relies on commitment from networks of colleagues;
• moves from individual experience through shared understanding to personal learning;
• expands the individual and collective skills of those who participate;
• models information-based learning;
• values personal experience but exposes it to a broader perspective;
• treats practical problems as worthy of research; and
• can be used to build bridges between researchers and practitioners.

During a time of change, the opportunity for school leaders to think about and debate their role becomes crucial if they are to be effective. To think that there is a clear, universal answer to the question of what constitutes an effective school leader is certainly unrealistic and inherently dangerous. The role of the head needs to be seen from an interactionist stance (Ball, 1987) and as something which is constantly subjected to critical review by both the individuals concerned and those who have an interest in their effectiveness. This must include those who are led. We believe that some of the techniques and analyses we used on our project can be used and developed by other groups to enable them to work towards that goal.

REFERENCES

Altricher, H., Posch, P. and Somekh, B. (1993) *Teachers Investigate their Work: An Introduction into Methods of Action Research*, Routledge, London.

Apple, M. (1993) Power, meaning and identity: critical sociology of education in the United States, *The British Journal of Sociology of Education*, Vol. 17, no. 2, pp. 125–144.

Ball, S. J., (1987) *The Micro-Politics of the School: Towards a Theory of School Organisation*, Methuen, London.

Carr, W. and Kemmis, S. (1986) *Becoming Critical. Education Knowledge and Action Research*, Deakin University Press, Geelong.

Connelly, F. and Clandinin, J. (1991) Narrative inquiry: stories from experience, in E. Short (ed.) *Forms of Curriculum Inquiry*, State University of New York Press, Albany.

Dunning, G. (1996) Management problems of new headteachers, *School Organisation*, Vol. 16, no. 1, pp. 111–128.

Goodson, I and Walker, R. (1991) (eds.) *Biography, Identity and Schooling*, Falmer, London.

Leithwood, K. A., Begley, P. and Cousins, J. (1992) *Developing Expert Leadership for Future Schools*, Falmer, Lewes.

Logan, L., Sachs, J. and Dempster, N. (1996) *Planning for Better Primary Schools*, The Australian College of Education, Canberra.

Mortimore, P., Sammons, P., Stoll, L., Lewis, D. and Ecob, E. (1988) *School Matters*, Open Books, Wells.

Reeves, J., Mahony, P. and Moos, L. (1997) Headship: issues of career, *Teacher Development*, Vol. 1, no. 1, pp. 43–56.

Weindling, D. and Earley, P. (1998) Heading for the top: the career paths of secondary heads, *Education Management and Administration*, Vol. 16, no. 1.

11

Postscript

Angus MacDonald

INTRODUCTION

It is, I think, both unusual and generous that the researchers in a project such as this should give the last word to a practitioner. It is an opportunity I am delighted to have because, for me, the experience of being part of this research project has been the intensely rewarding one of being involved in a whole series of rich dialogues. There has been, for example, a dialogue between those outside school leadership looking in and those involved in school leadership looking out. There has also been a dialogue between those involved in school leadership in different countries and in different systems. There has been too a dialogue within myself between the insights, perceptions and analyses that emerged and my own practice, experience and understanding of school leadership.

It is from these discussions that this chapter has emerged. Some of the thoughts on leadership may be able to be generalised to any situation, others will apply more specifically to leadership as it is exercised in a school setting. The chapter itself is also an exploration of the many interactions that take place in the leadership situation. I have suggested three kinds of interactions: first, the internal dialogue within the leader between his or her knowledge and his or her awareness of that knowledge; second, the dialogue between the leader and those whom he or she leads through the consultation processes commonly used in schools; and third, the potential conflict between the leader's aims and others' expectations in the use of these processes.

I hope that what follows is recognisable to all who reflect on school leadership, practitioners and researchers alike, and gives a brief taste to the reader of the richness of the many exchanges that took place in the course of the project.

METACOGNITION

Metacognition, if by that we mean our awareness of our own state of knowledge, is a good, if rather unlikely, last word. It would be an unremarkable statement to say that leaders in schools, as in other situations and organisations, rely upon their knowledge in making judgements and decisions. The difference between good and successful leaders and those who are less so may depend in part at least upon their awareness of the state of their knowledge. The following small grid may help to illustrate the point made above. The title 'The MacDonald Management Metacognition Matrix', may be altogether too grandiose. In the grid, the horizontal axis refers to the leader's state of knowledge in relation to any situation or decision, while the vertical axis refers to his or her awareness of that state of knowledge.

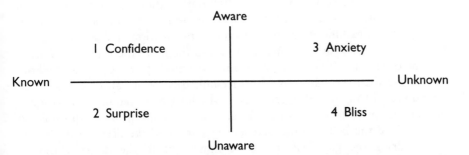

It is surely good leadership and good management to be as knowledgeable as possible about any decision or situation. The greater the degree of certainty, and the more one is aware of that, the greater the confidence of the leadership. The first quadrant, then, is labelled Confidence; this is the state of mind where the leader is aware that his or her knowledge is sound and sufficient to form the necessary judgement, or make the necessary decisions. Those looking at leadership from the outside often take the commonsense view that this is how decisions are made. The leader waits until he or she is aware that they have sufficient knowledge and then decides. Those involved in leadership know that only very seldom are they allowed this luxury and that to seek this state before making a decision would, in practice, be the paralysis of leadership. Most often, decisions and judgements have to be made in very different conditions.

Leaders quite often make decisions and judgements in the condition of Surprise; this is an ability much admired and valued by others. In this condition, the leaders surprise themselves. It occurs where a new situation has arisen and the leader is surprised to find himself or herself reacting with a sense of sureness of touch, of knowing just what to do and then doing it. It is as though the leader was unaware of what he or she knew until the situation itself demanded the response and he found it already formed. It may be to do with unarticulated knowledge, or it may be to do with the ability to see through the detail of the situation to the fundamental issues, and then to apply the relevant principles to produce a resolution. Whatever, it is much prized by others because it conveys a sense of ability to 'think on one's feet', or of a very profound depth of experience. It inspires confidence and trust. For this reason, the wise leader will keep his or her sense of surprise well hidden and will look exactly as they would have, had they been aware of this all along. On the face of it, this quadrant is indistinguishable from the first quadrant in practice. Perhaps this is why it is so seldom acknowledged.

The third quadrant is that of Anxiety, the condition in which leaders feel that most decisions and judgements are made. Most situations will not permit a leader the time to find out about all the things about which he or she does not know The shrewd leader will, of course, reduce the uncertainty as far possible; beyond that, the leader will consult (to try to gain more information, but also to spread ownership of the 'fall-out' if things go wrong), develop fall-back positions and stage his or her commitment to the decision so that there is some flexibility to respond as more information emerges. But always the degree of uncertainty creates anxiety and the more the leader is aware of what he or she does not know, the greater the anxiety will be. This condition also can lead to the paralysis of leadership, because it can of course affect the individual to a major degree; this is why leadership requires real courage. One of the most difficult tasks a leader has is to sustain both flexibility of response and the belief in the outcome that inspired the decision in the first place, during the gap between the commitment to the decision and the realisation of the outcome itself. Anything that goes wrong within this time gap, however unconnected it may seem to be, tends to be linked to the original decision, especially if it were contentious. The leader must uphold and defend the decision while bearing in mind the possibility that the connection might, in truth, be there.

The fourth quadrant, Bliss, is the most interesting one because this is the condition in which all decisions and judgements are truly made. Awareness of lack of knowledge is Anxiety; lack of awareness of lack of knowledge is Bliss. The trouble, however, with being unaware of what we need to know, and do not know, is that we lack both prompt and motive to make us find out. As leaders – as human beings – we are always in this situation; we can never be sure that we are aware of all that we need to know, whether we actually know it or not. If this were a Mediaeval Management Matrix, this quadrant would be clearly marked 'Terra Incognita' and 'Here be Monsters' for this is truly unknown territory and monsters do lurk here – the monstrously unlucky, the monstrously unlikely and the monstrously unfair – and they can take any form. Every leader carries this 'Terra Incognita' into every situation, however familiar, or new, it may appear; this condition is so all-pervading and permanent that we cease to recognise it and we operate in practice often as though it does not exist. Perhaps this is necessary or else leadership would really be paralysed; except that good leadership allows for it and takes action.

The good leader will look more widely and think harder about possible consequences of any decision, but probably there is only one set of activities available to leaders to help them map at least some of the 'Terra Incognita' they know must be there and to identify the monsters that might lurk within. This is one reason for the importance of consultation and the bringing of different views, sets of knowledge and experiences to bear on an issue or problem as a leadership activity. It is, however, not the only one. There is always an element of consent involved in leadership. Our managers are appointed by due process, but we choose to invest our trust, belief and confidence in our leaders. Consultation is the means by which this consent is maintained, with our loss of trust in our leaders often the reason for its withdrawal. It is hard for someone who knows something as a simple matter of fact to appreciate that his or her leader does not know it. It is harder still for that person to appreciate that the leader is not aware that he does not know it, but completely impossible for him to understand why he was not asked. Consultation is therefore an essential leadership activity and it is an interesting question indeed to consider why, even when entered into with goodwill on all sides, it so often goes awry.

It is perhaps not sufficiently appreciated that consultation is not a single, unitary process. There are different types of consultation, each appropriate to its own range of issues, each offering different levels of involvement, methods and expectations. The bitter rejection of consultation as a sham in which the decision was already made and in which views offered were ignored is much more to do with inappropriate expectations than with personal pique or management manipulation. For consultation to succeed and to support leadership it must have the right climate of expectation of awareness of method and of level of involvement. Without these preconditions, staff will almost inevitably be disappointed and disillusioned by the consultation process.

The model of consultation which might be termed 'inclusive' is the one that springs most readily to mind when the process of consultation is discussed. Here the expectation is that all members of a school staff will be consulted by having their views sought individually. There is often also an expectation that the decision will be made on the basis of the majority view. This, indeed, can be the case, where, for example, voluntary input is sought from staff – a school activities week, for example. In such a case, it would be wise to base a decision on more than a simple majority and to have obtained prior agreement from staff that all would support the decision reached by the agreed method. An activities week will not work if twenty-five per cent of the staff do not support it. Other issues affecting the whole staff can be decided in this way, even where the basic decision is imposed. In relation to a national curricular initiative, the decision is not whether or not the school will implement it, but how. Staff always appreciate being involved in decisions such as phasing, resourcing and the development of appropriate staff structures, but only if they are clear in the first place about the nature of the decision.

The methods used in this kind of consultation are familiar to schools – whole-staff meetings, questionnaires, written responses from groups of staff and individual interviews. Their disadvantages are well rehearsed. They may in turn be daunting and inhibiting for many individuals, paper-driven, time-consuming and difficult to construct if a valid and reliable response is sought.

Inclusive consultation addresses issues that affect the whole staff and acknowledges their fundamental professional equality. Those who argue that all consultation should take this form have not, however, acknowledged its weaknesses. Above all, it cannot deliver discretion or confidentiality. This is not the kind of consultation that most would welcome where, for example, a headteacher is preparing a report or reference in relation to an application for promotion. Nor is this the only situation in which a headteacher or leader within a school may wish to consult, but with discretion. It is often necessary to gauge the reaction of staff to a proposal or development that may be contentious because quite often the way such an issue is introduced will have a major bearing on the reaction it receives. For this kind of consultation, where discretion or confidentiality are required, a selective approach is often used and the leader chooses the individuals to be consulted. This method saves time and work for the majority while targeting those who, through their skill, knowledge or experience, have a particular contribution to make. Its dangers are that it can be seen to be, and in truth can actually be, manipulative and biased, favouring some individuals and points of view as against others. It is, after all, only human to enjoy the reassurance and confirmation of speaking to others of a like mind. It is worth also noting in passing that the majority of staff is unaware that such consultation has taken place.

Representative consultation, on the other hand, gives the full group being consulted a degree of participation in the selection of those who are to be actively involved in the consultation process. This may be done by the election of representatives by staff of a school, or through seeking volunteers or nominees to fill an agreed structure which is in some way representative of the whole staff. For example, this may be someone to represent each of the main curricular areas or someone to represent each level of staff. Groups such as this undoubtedly save time and workload for the majority of staff and they can represent a wide range of views, skills, interests and knowledge. They can, however, also be prone to being hijacked by a particular interest group, or even to being dominated by a single individual. They can also, if they are not time-limited, become rigid and routine. If they do not keep in touch with their constituencies, they become out of touch with the staff as a whole. Unless such groups maintain a good two-way flow of information between themselves and their constituencies, they run the risk of providing misleading guidance to the school leader, while leaving the staff as a whole feeling that its voice has never been heard. In such a situation, staff will feel at best that the consultation process has broken down and at worst that it has actively excluded them.

It is, however, in the moment of crisis, the time of emergency, that the heroic qualities of the leader as an individual are most needed, most visible and most appreciated. This is the point at which consultation procedures are seen to be both inappropriate and burdensome and our hero moves swiftly and single-handedly to meet and resolve the crisis that has arisen. In fact, of course, what really happens is rather different. In a time of crisis, the school leader is much more likely to indulge in a swift piece of selective consultation. The choice of individuals consulted will be governed by speed of availability, as well as by ability to contribute. The leader will generally have some strategy as to how to proceed forming in his or her mind and this will be 'bounced off' the chosen group, while also taking other ideas and strategies into account. At this stage, an entirely different strategy for dealing with the crisis could emerge. If appropriate, the staff will be informed of what has happened, the need for speed of reaction will be explained and staff will be told how matters will be dealt with and what they should do. Once the immediate crisis has passed, the school leader will then set in motion a process of inclusive consultation, debriefing staff, checking on the effect of the decisions made and making adjustments where appropriate. Finally, once matters have been fully resolved, staff will be informed and the situation will be returned to normal. It is a most curious contradiction that it is in serious situations of this kind which affect the whole organisation that staff most expect to be kept fully informed, yet the leader of the school or organisation is most perceived to be acting alone. Perhaps it is the very high profile the leader must take, combined with the fact that the 'normal' processes of consultation do not happen in the expected order, that leads to these apparently contradictory views.

School leadership is very much more than the passive acceptance of staff that they must do as the headteacher says simply because the individual concerned has been appointed to that position. A school leader, at any level in the organisation, has won the trust, belief and confidence of staff to a significant degree and these are assets which the staff has given to the leader. Where there is merely passive acceptance, these assets are substantially withheld and where there is perceived betrayal, disappointment or loss of confidence, these assets can be withdrawn. Consultation is the main means by which the leader in a school, or any organisation, maintains the consent of staff to the trusteeship of these assets, as well as the main means by which the leader reduces and maps the 'Terra Incognita' which he or she carries into any and every situation. The conclusion must therefore be to emphasise the importance of consultation even where the last word for school managers is 'metacognition'.

Subject Index

Author Index